THE SCOURGE OF
MONETARISM

THE SCOURGE OF MONETARISM

PART I

The Radcliffe Report and Monetary Policy
The Radcliffe Lectures
delivered at the University of Warwick
1981

PART II

Monetary Policy in the United Kingdom
Evidence to the Treasury
and Civil Service Committee
July 1980

NICHOLAS KALDOR

OXFORD UNIVERSITY PRESS
1982

Oxford University Press, Walton Street, Oxford OX2 6DP

London Glasgow New York Toronto
Delhi Bombay Calcutta Madras Karachi
Kuala Lumpur Singapore Hong Kong Tokyo
Nairobi Dar es Salaam Cape Town
Melbourne Auckland

and associate companies in
Beirut Berlin Ibadan Mexico City

Published in the United States by
Oxford University Press, New York

British Library Cataloguing in Publication Data

Kaldor, Nicholas Kaldor, Baron
The scourge of monetarism. – (Radcliffe lectures)
1. Quantity theory of money
I. Title   II. Series
332.4   HG221
ISBN 0-19-877187-8

Library of Congress Cataloging in Publication Data

Kaldor, Nicholas, 1908–
The scourge of monetarism.
(Radcliffe lectures)
1. Monetary policy.   2. Monetary policy – Great
Britain.   3. Chicago school of economics.   I. Title.
II. Series.
HG230.3.K34   332.4'6   82-6380
ISBN 0-19-877187-8 (pbk.)   AACR2

Typeset by Anne Joshua Associates, Oxford
Printed in Great Britain by Billing and Sons Ltd.,
London, Oxford and Worcester

CONTENTS

LIST OF FIGURES AND TABLES

FIGURES

TABLES

INTRODUCTION

It is the second time this century that monetarist dogma has become the official creed of the Government of Britain. The first occasion was in the 1920s when, egged on by the Cunliffe Committee and pressures from the City, Britain was driven to return to the Gold Standard at the pre-war parity — despite, as we now know, the opposition, if not the hostility, of the then Chancellor of the Exchequer, Winston Churchill. The disastrous consequences, and the reactionary character of this step were brilliantly analysed in a pamphlet by Keynes (a pamphlet far ahead of the times and ahead of much of his own future writing on the subject), in which he branded monetary policy as 'simply a campaign against the standard of life of the working classes', operating through the 'deliberate intensification of unemployment . . . by using the weapon of economic necessity against individuals and against particular industries — a policy which the country would never permit if it knew what was being done'.[1] As the decade wore on, resistance to any 'reflationary' policy intensified. The 'Treasury view' of the 1920s was no more nor less profound than the present views of Mrs Thatcher.

But in 1931 Britain was saved from the horrors of monetarism against her will. The maintenance of the Gold Standard was regarded as the supreme objective, for the sake of which a group of right-wing Labour Ministers, led by the Prime Minister, Ramsay MacDonald, deserted the Party and formed the National Government. But despite the highly deflationary budget which the new Government hastily introduced — more deflationary, in comparable terms, than the present Government's recent efforts — the Gold Standard could not be saved.

And with its abandonment, on 18 September 1931, the rule of monetarism came to an abrupt end. The Bank Rate was reduced almost overnight from 6 per cent to 2 per cent, the new Chancellor, Neville Chamberlain, carried out the greatest conversion operation in history (the reduction of the interest on the War Loan from 5 per cent to $3\frac{1}{2}$ per cent, which brought down the whole structure of long-term interest rates) and introduced a protective tariff on all manufactured goods which led to the fastest rate of economic growth in British history.

[1] J. M. Keynes, *The Economic Consequences of Mr. Churchill* (London, 1925), reprinted in the *Collected Writings of John Maynard Keynes* Vol. IX (London, 1972), pp. 207–30.

The appearance of Keynes's *General Theory* in 1936 gave the cheap money policy its theoretical underpinning. The policy of low interest rates was maintained throughout the war — the Government borrowed enormous sums, at very low interest rates, not only on short-term but also in medium and long-term paper, without the slightest difficulty — and in 1944 the Coalition Government pledged itself to the maintenance of 'high and stable' levels of employment after the war — an undertaking which would have been inconceivable in the pre-war era and particularly when the country was under the Gold Standard.

The six years of the Attlee Government, which succeeded the Coalition Government in the summer of 1945, were undoubtedly the most successful of this century in terms of economic and social achievement. The retention of the wartime system of controls made it possible to avoid the reconversion crisis and the heavy unemployment which followed in the wake of the First World War. The level of industrial investment, as a percentage of the GDP, was doubled as compared to pre-war, and the Utopian-sounding export target of 75 per cent above 1938 was approximately attained by 1950, when UK exports of manufactures accounted for 25.5 per cent of world exports — the highest percentage since 1913.[2]

However, during all these years, the banks and the financial institutions of the City were increasingly unhappy. The profits of the clearing banks were severely cut by Hugh Dalton's reduction of the interest paid to banks on Government borrowing from 2 per cent to one-half of one per cent; the Stock Exchange was stagnant owing to the dividend freeze, the control over new issues and investment abroad; building controls prevented property speculation. All this unhappiness was reflected in an increasing clamour (mainly led by financial journalists) for the reactivation of monetary policy as a superior method of dealing with inflation (which was held down quite successfully, until the outbreak of the Korean War, by Stafford Cripps's incomes policy) and as a means of introducing greater flexibility and compeitition into the economy.

The new Tory administration of November 1951 was pledged to liquidate wartime 'austerity', to restore life to the City by abolishing controls, and to reactivate the Bank Rate as an instrument of monetary

---

[2] From then on Britain's share in world exports began to decline, partly on account of 'supply-side' difficulties in the engineering industries, caused by the pre-emption of capacity for rearmament purposes, and partly on account of the rapid expansion of German and Japanese production and exports.

policy. It proceeded cautiously at first, and the sudden collapse of prices with the end of the post-Korean-War scare made it appear that monetary controls were indeed highly efficacious. But that was short-lived. A boom developed in the years 1954–6 which the authorities were quite powerless to control. These troubles were ascribed, however, not to the ineffectiveness of monetary policy but only to the ineffective manner in which the policy was operated (whether on account of ignorance or the lack of suitable instruments or institutions). This was to be remedied by a grand inquiry into the workings of the monetary system – the Radcliffe Committee – whose report is the subject-matter of the lectures reproduced in the first part of this volume.

The unanimous Report of the Radcliffe Committee, issued in the summer of 1959, represented a serious set-back to monetarism. For the Report, much to everyone's surprise and in clear contrast to all previous grand Committees of Inquiry on the subject (such as Cunliffe's or Macmillan's), declined to accord any importance to the money supply or its changes, and asserted that 'in ordinary times' monetary policy cannot play more than a 'subordinate part' in guiding the economy. All this represented a clear break with the classical monetarist tradition of Britain, a total rejection of the ideas of the Friedmanites (who by that time were making a lot of noise and spreading out fanwise from Chicago), and the re-affirmation of Keynesian principles of economic management, which continued to dominate the British scene (barring, perhaps, a brief interval between Mr Heath's acceptance of the Selsdon programme in 1970 and his rejection of it in 1971).

However, the steady rise in the importance of the City and its institutions (measured, for example, by the increasing amount of space taken up by the financial or business pages of newspapers), the growing influence and prestige of financial journalists and of stockbrokers' circulars, supplemented by the floods of increasingly obscurantist literature from America, generated a new epidemic of monetarism of a more virulent kind, which engulfed the right wing of the Tory Party and, for a period, the right wing of the Labour Party too.

The distinguishing mark of this new wave of monetarism is its extreme dogmatism and complete lack of intellectual coherence.[3]

---

[3] For that reason, despite strong temptations, the new creed made comparatively few converts among academic economists, as shown by the Manifesto signed by 364 University teachers in economics in March 1981 – and the absence of any counter-manifesto in support of the Government's policies.

When Mrs Thatcher's Government came to power bold assertions were made in official publications as well as in ministerial speeches which marked a sharp break with past traditions. The exponents of the Government's policy have shown themselves quite incapable of familiariz-ing themselves with the most elementary official statistics, and have kept repeating, parrot-fashion, statements which manifestly did not follow from their own premises.

It was perhaps this very ignorance which made them so willing to make so many bold predictions. They regarded inflation as an auto-matic and inevitable consequence of an increase in the money supply; the latter in turn was the inevitable consequence of the public sector deficit, which in turn was an adjunct of Keynesian policies of 'demand management'. They set themselves precise targets in terms of the PSBR, the money supply, the reduction in the tax burden, and the reduction of inflation, first for one year, and then, in their much publicized 'medium term strategy', for a four-year period, 1980–3. So far, they have failed on every count – the money supply on their own chosen definition (£M3) rose much faster than before (by 18 per cent a year since they took office, as against the 11 per cent a year experienced in the previous two years, and set by them as their own maximum target); inflation doubled (to 22 per cent) in their first year;[4] the PSBR turned out to be 50 per cent higher than planned. The examples could be multiplied. But none of this has caused Mrs Thatcher and her band of close supporters to bat an eyelid. On the contrary, as time has passed, they appear to have become increasingly confident of success. The true reason, one can surmise, lies in their success in transforming the labour market from a twentieth-century sellers' market to a nineteenth-century buyers' market, with wholesome effects on factory discipline, wage claims, and proneness to strike. But the cost has been horrendous in terms of loss output, loss of social cohesion, and sheer misery of the unemployed, particularly the young.

And, contrary to the claims of Ministers, it was quite unnecessary. The twenty-five post-war years of full employment have demonstrated that it is possible to run the economy at high levels of capacity utiliza-tion, with higher levels of output and a higher productivity growth than could have been obtained by pre-war financial or monetary policies. However, as a result of the monetarism of the Austrian, rather than the Chicagoan, variety (represented by the writings of Professors

---

[4] It has since come down to 12 per cent – which is still higher than the rate prevailing when they took office.

Hayek and Mises), a group of Conservatives led by Sir Keith Joseph convinced themselves around 1974 that only a prolonged period of retreat and retrenchment could save the country. 'There is no other possible economic policy that an honourable Government could have introduced given the appalling long-term structural problems of the economy.'[5]

The 'appalling long-term structural problems' consisted of the decline of British manufacturing industry relative to that of her competitors, which greatly ante-dates the post World War II period, and was most eloquently described by Joseph Chamberlain during his famous tariff reform campaign in 1902.

So Britain's problems could hardly have been ascribed to Keynes, Beveridge, or the rejection of monetarism after 1932: as economic historians confirm, Britain enjoyed a higher rate of prosperity and improvement in living standards in the years of Keynesian demand-management than in any comparable period in her history. In fact, Britain's de-industrialization was much aggravated by Mrs Thatcher's policies, although the full consequences of this are masked (and for some time will continue to be masked) by our unexpected fortune in the discovery of North Sea oil. The Government's reliance on 'market forces', combined with the severe deflationary policies pursued through higher taxes and interest rates, have meant that the benefit which should have been derived from oil has been very largely wasted. It helped us to make huge capital exports and thereby to build up the industrial capacity of other countries but not of Britain.[6] When the present policies are finally abandoned (whether by the Conservatives or their opponents) the 'supply side' of the British economy will be found to have shrunk a great deal. The numerous factory closures which have *not* been balanced by the building of new factories, the roads and houses which have *not* been built, the social infrastructure (including higher education) which has been allowed to deteriorate are losses which can never be recouped — however much present

---

[5] See the Hon. Archibald Hamilton, MP, *The Times*, 26 January 1982.

[6] The assertion often made by the Government that Britain's recession and unemployment were mainly caused by the world-wide recession, and that they were 'only a little more severe' than those of Germany, France, and other EEC countries, leaves out of account that whilst Britain *benefited* from the rise in oil prices — and was therefore better able to follow policies of internal expansion and enlarged investment, without being limited by a balance of payments constraint — the other countries suffered from a deterioration of their terms of trade, causing severe balance of payments deficit which made it impossible for them to follow more intensive reflationary policies.

policies are put into reverse, the real income of Britain at any particular future date will always be lower than it would have been if the Thatcher experiment had never taken place.

When, after the first year, it appeared evident to most people that the monetarist policies of Mrs Thatcher were not working, the newly formed Select Committee of the House of Commons on the Treasury and the Civil Service ordered an inquiry into monetary policy. The invitation extended to me to give evidence on this broad subject gave me an opportunity to deal with the contentions of the monetarists, British and foreign, in some detail. Though this paper appeared in one of the Committee's numerous Minutes of Evidence, I have been urged to reproduce it here so as to make it more readily available.[7]

February 1982   Nicholas Kaldor

---

[7] This paper written in May–June 1980 is reproduced in Part II without any attempt to bring the various figures, etc., up to date, though a few stylistic improvements have been made, and minor inaccuracies corrected. Where the current situation (in February 1982) departs in some important respect from the situation described in the text, an addition enclosed in square brackets is made in the text, or a reference mark (*, †, etc.) refers the reader to a note on p. 112.

PART I

The Radcliffe Report and Monetary Policy

*The Radcliffe Lectures
delivered at the University of Warwick
1981*

A PERSONAL NOTE ON LORD RADCLIFFE

The publication of these lectures gives me an opportunity to pay tribute to one of the most remarkable men whom I had the good fortune to encounter in the course of a long professional life. Lord Radcliffe became Chairman of the Royal Commission on Taxation of Profits and Income (which *preceded* the Committee on the Working of the Monetary System) at an early stage in the life of that Commission, of which I was a member, and this brought me into contact with a truly exceptional mind; he had the rare quality of making one feel on the top of one's form in discussions with him. Lord Radcliffe was a lawyer, not an economist, but the subject-matter of the Commission's work, the principles of taxation, involved economic theory at an intricate level and in its most variegated aspects. Lord Radcliffe's capacity to absorb the methods of reasoning of economics struck me on many occasions as astonishing, and this personal judgement was in no way impaired by the fact that we fundamentally differed on what economists call value-judgements — that is, the political objectives which the chosen system of taxation should serve. Radcliffe was a Conservative in the best English sense of that term — he cared very much about liberty and he believed that liberty and fair treatment can only be secured by stable institutions and particularly by stable laws which define and circumscribe the limits of individual freedom in relation to society. I, on the other hand, was deeply convinced that the ultimate objective of policy must comprise equality as well as freedom; and that a system of taxation should aim at fairness not only as between different individuals in the same economic circumstances but also as between individuals in different circumstances — between rich and poor, between capitalists and workers. This meant that in the end I was constrained to write a minority report — despite the fact that we worked together closely and harmoniously over years, reviewing the complex technical aspects and anomalies of the tax system.

From that point of view it is a matter of regret that our collaboration should have been on the tax commission and not on Lord Radcliffe's second great Committee of Enquiry, on the Working of the Monetary System — when there would have been no such differences between us in terms of either means or ends. This is shown by the fact — to which Roy Harrod has drawn attention[1] — that the views put forward in the Committee's Report bear, as Harrod put it, 'a certain family resemblance on critical issues' to the arguments and conclusions put forward in my memorandum prepared at the request of the Committee in June 1958.[2]

[1] *Economic Journal*, December 1965, pp. 796–7.

[2] This has been reprinted in my *Collected Economic Essays*, Vol. III (London, 1964, repr. 1978).

LECTURE I

As these lectures are intended to commemorate the late Lord Radcliffe, who was the first Chancellor of this University, it is particularly fitting that I should take as my starting-point for an analysis of the current state of monetary theory the Report of the *Committee on the Working of the Monetary System*[1] of which Lord Radcliffe was the Chairman and (to my knowledge) also the principal author. Since there cannot be many of the present generation of students who have read the Report or are familiar with the circumstances which gave rise to it, it is best to begin with the historical background. The cheap money era which began with the Great Depression and the abandonment of the Gold Standard meant that monetary policy was in abeyance from 1932, right through the war period and the post-war period following until the return of a Conservative Government in November 1951.

During the war the Bank Rate remained at 2 per cent and the rates of gilt-edged were equally stabilized at low levels through the open market operations of the Bank which were extended to all maturities. The Government financed the war largely through the issue of Treasury Bills and to a lesser extent through the issue of short- and medium-term bonds. But the Government also saw to it that the banking system redeposited its surplus of investible funds with the Treasury, thereby limiting the amount of credit that could be extended to the private sector. This system was maintained after the war, when, thanks to the return of a Labour Government, strongly under the influence of Keynesian principles, the Chancellor of the Exchequer relied on fiscal policy to maintain full employment and to avoid an excessive pressure of demand. Interest rates were kept at a minimum — the interest paid on Treasury deposits receipts (as distinct from Treasury Bills) was reduced by Hugh Dalton from 2 per cent to one-half of one per cent whilst long-term issues were made (up to 1947) at 2 to $2\frac{1}{2}$ per cent. This was during a period when the rate of inflation fluctuated around 4 to 5 per cent.

But throughout these years, and particularly after 1947, there was growing agitation for the reactivation of monetary policy, which, it was claimed, provided a far more flexible instrument of economic control than fiscal policy. The first tentative changes introduced by

[1] Cmnd. 827 (HMSO, August 1959).

the new Chancellor, Mr — now Lord — Butler, in November 1951 were modest. The Bank Rate was raised from 2 to $2\frac{1}{2}$ per cent but it was accompanied by a special re-discount on Treasury Bills which meant that the rate on them was kept one-half per cent *below* the Bank Rate instead of one-half per cent above it as had been the case previously. However, in the Budget of 1952, Bank Rate was raised to 4 per cent, though this was reduced later to $3\frac{1}{2}$ per cent and then to 3 per cent in the course of 1954. When, towards the end of 1954, the authorities became aware that an excessive pressure of demand was developing, a tightening of both fiscal and monetary measures would have been called for if the policy had been followed through. However, the Budget of 1955, introduced one month before a General Election, actually cut income by 6*d*. arguing that 'taking into account the resources of a flexible monetary policy' a tight fiscal policy was no longer so necessary as it was earlier.

As it happened, this juxtaposition of fiscal relaxation and monetary tightening provided the first real test of the efficacy of monetary measures. There was a succession of increases in the Bank Rate in the course of 1955 and immediately after, but bank advances continued to rise sharply, despite an increasing crescendo of warnings culminating in an unprecedented direct request from the Chancellor of the Exchequer to the clearing banks in July for 'a positive and significant reduction in their advances over the next few months'. Despite this request bank advances continued to rise stubbornly, and by October the Chancellor felt obliged to introduce an autumn Budget which more than reversed the fiscal relaxation of the April Budget through an increase in indirect taxes and the profit tax, and by cutting public investment programmes. But bank advances continued to expand until the second half of 1956, and were then halted as a result of the introduction of direct controls on bank advances — though this did not diminish the growing pressure on resources.

The experience of these years made it clear that monetary policy measures were not working as intended. And the blame was laid, as on many subsequent occasions, not on a failure of basic design or basic theory, but on inadequate methods of control or lack of competence in operating them. Hence in May 1957, a highly powered Committee was appointed with wide-ranging terms of reference 'to inquire into the working of the monetary and credit system and to make recommendations', the first of its kind since the Macmillan Committee reported in 1931. The Committee was a small one — eight members and the Chairman; it contained two leading economists, Professor Sayers and Professor Cairncross, as well as a number of distinguished public figures, among them Sir Oliver Franks, now Lord Franks, and Lord Harcourt. Their report was unanimous, without a single reservation by any of its members, and the work was completed in just over two years, despite the fact that the Committee took oral evidence which amounted to nearly a thousand foolscap pages in print, and digested 150 memoranda from institutions and individuals which took up a further 750 foolscap pages.

This was a remarkable achievement — all the more remarkable because on the central issues the Committee took up a position that was the very opposite of the orthodox or the traditional view. Their main concern, it is clear, was to review the existing institutional framework and the manner of operation of controls over demand through the monetary and banking system, and to make recommendations of how that system could be improved. This required a detailed description of the complex pattern of financial institutions, a review of the existing instruments of monetary control, a historical survey of its effectiveness in the post-war period, and finally, an examination, albeit a cursory one, of the underlying theory concerning the role of money in the economy.

For those chiefly instrumental in the decision to set up the Committee, the Report must have come as something of an anticlimax. For on the most important policy issues the Committee clearly took a negative view. Their review of the monetary policy of the 1950s amounts to a severe condemnation.

We are driven to the conclusion that the more conventional instruments have failed to keep the system in smooth balance, but that every now and again the mounting pressure of demand has in one way or another . . . driven the Government to take action, and that the quick results thus required have been mainly concentrated on the hire purchase front and on investment in the public sector which could be cut by administrative decisions. . . . That these two should be the 'residuary legatees' for real resources when sharp adjustments were called for is not a comforting thought. It is far removed from the smooth and widespread adjustment sometimes claimed as the virtue of monetary action; this is no gentle hand on the steering wheel which keeps a well driven car in its right place on the road.[2]

[2] Ibid., para. 472.

And as for the future,

we envisage the use of monetary measures as not in ordinary times playing other than a subordinate part in guiding the development of the economy. . . . when all has been said on the possibility of monetary action and of its likely efficacy, our conclusion is that monetary measures cannot alone be relied upon to keep in nice balance an economy subject to major strains from both without and within. Monetary measures can help, but that is all.[3]

This negative attitude is reflected in their concrete recommendations which are few and far between.

It will be seen that our review of monetary measures has not led us to any positive and simple recommendations. No method, new or old, provides the remedy for all our troubles. We do not find any solution of the problem of influencing total demand in more violent manipulation of interest rates; we find control of the supply of money to be no more than an important facet of debt management; we cannot recommend any substantial changes in the rules under which banks operate; we do not regard the capital issues control as useful in ordinary times; and we believe there are narrow limits to the usefulness of hire purchase controls.[4]

Their concrete recommendation was that more statistical information be regularly provided by the Bank of England, more research be undertaken on the behaviour of various monetary magnitudes in relation to each other, and finally that the co-ordination of policies between the Treasury and the Bank of England be improved through the formation of a new high-level Committee for this purpose. All this has since been done. Finally they gave their reluctant blessing to the use of 'emergency measures' (such as direct controls on the expansion of bank advances) in 'emergencies', though the causes of such 'emergencies', and the ways of avoiding them, received very little attention.

As the Committee was aware, the influence of monetary policy can be looked upon in two ways. One is through the control over the extension of bank credit, which was traditionally operated through the Bank Rate and the open market operations of the Central Bank, but was supplemented, in the latter half of the 1950s, by quantitative controls over bank credit.

The Committee found that while the policy created a 'diffused difficulty of borrowing' by 'driving frustrated borrowers to other

---

[3] Ibid., paras. 511 and 514.   [4] Ibid., para. 514.

sources of credit, where borrowing was more expensive and sometimes more onerous in other ways',[5] this had no important effect on the pressure of demand in the economy, though it had highly undesirable effects on particular industries, 'among them new and progressive branches of light engineering. These industries complain that their production schedules are expensively dislocated and that the forward planning so necessary for efficient production has been made almost intolerably difficult.'[6]

They sum up their conclusions as follows:

(1) the obstruction to particular channels of finance have had *no* effect on the pressure of total demand, but have made for much inefficiency in financial organisation; (2) that the controls of hire purchase terms have had sizeable impact, of a once-and-for-all kind, on each major change; and (3) that these sizeable effects on total demand have implied major directional effects which, though sometimes deliberately sought, have in general been detrimental to industrial efficiency.[7]

As to the future, both the review of historical experience and the evidence submitted to them made the Committee thoroughly pessimistic. Credit policy through the Bank's determination of the short rates of interest was supposed to operate on a particular form of investment, namely stock-building. A study of post-war national income figures revealed that stock-building was the one really unstable source of demand in the economy, and one which was difficult to control except through the instrument of credit policy. Ever since the writings of Hawtrey, credit control through interest rates appeared to economists the ideal form of smoothing out fluctuations in stock-building. However the Committee unexpectedly found that 'stocks of commodities are *extremely insensitive* to interest rates, and in any case they are often financed with long-term capital and could be much more widely so if firms found this much cheaper. It is at fixed capital that the rate of interest must strike if it is to have any direct impact' — meaning, presumably, long term investment. In fact, because borrowers and lenders can easily switch between the short end and the long end of the market, 'expectations of fluctuating long rates would necessitate even wider fluctuations in short rates . . . causing much larger swings than hitherto in long-term rates of interest . . . This course appears to us as probably impracticable and certainly so disadvantageous as to warrant our ruling it out as a general line of policy'.[8] A further reason to which the Committee attached importance was that 'the intricate and highly developed network of financial institutions bases some of its strength on the existence of a large body of highly marketable Government bonds whose market values are assumed to have a considerable degree of stability. . . . For these reasons we reject any suggestion that the rate of interest weapon should be made more effective by being used much more violently than hitherto'.[9]

So much for monetary policy looked on as an instrument of regulating demand through *credit control*. But the Committee was aware that there is another case for the use of monetary policy, based not on credit control but on control over 'the supply of money', which is seen 'by those who hold views of this kind' as 'a quantity which governs the demand for real goods and services', and which — though the Report is somewhat obscure on this point — constitutes a *distinct* source of demand additional to that derived from 'the flow of money incomes'.

It is for this reason that some experts consider that the central task of monetary authorities is to keep a tight control on the supply of money. If, it is argued, the central bank has both the will and the means to control the supply of money, and either keeps it fixed or allows it to increase only in step with the growing needs of a growing economy, all will be well. In its extreme form, this doctrine perhaps is not widely held in this country [the recent manifesto of 364 economists shows that it is *still* not 'widely held'] but its more moderate versions, according to all of which the concept of the supply of money holds the key position, are commonly heard, and were put in evidence before us.

Our view is different. Though we do not regard the supply of money as an unimportant quantity, we view it as only part of a wider structure of liquidity in the economy . . . *It is the whole liquidity position* that is relevant to spending decisions and our interest in the supply of money is due to its significance in the whole liquidity picture. . . .

The decision to spend thus depends upon liquidity in the broad sense, not upon immediate access to the money. . . . The spending is not limited by the amount of money in existence but it is related to the amount of money people think they can get hold of, whether by receipts of income (for instance from sales) by disposal of capital assets or by borrowing.[10]

[8] Ibid., paras. 489–90, italics added.   [9] Ibid., para. 491.
[10] Ibid., paras. 388–90, italics added.

But the key to their attitude is found in the next paragraph.

The fact that spending is not limited by the amount of money in existence is sometimes argued by reference to the velocity of circulation of money. It is possible for example to demonstrate statistically that during the last few years the volume of spending has greatly increased while the supply of money has hardly changed; the velocity of circulation of money has increased. We have not made more use of this concept because we cannot find any reason for supposing, or any experience in monetary history indicating, that there is any limit to the velocity of circulation; it is a statistical concept that tells us nothing directly of the motivation that influences the level of total demand.[11]

They add in a footnote 'that the more efficient the financial structure, the more can the velocity of circulation be stretched without serious inconvenience being caused.'[12]

I wonder whether the members of the Committee were fully aware that in one sentence, or part of a sentence, they repudiated in one fell swoop the quantity theory of money in all its versions, from Cantillon and Hume, through Ricardo, Marshall, and Walras, Irving Fisher and Milton Friedman (to mention only the most prominent) with their army of camp followers, right down to Mrs Thatcher.

For it is the essence of the quantity theory of money that the demand for money, whether expressed as an amount of real purchasing power, a potential basket of goods over which an individual wishes to keep command in the form of money, or as a proportion of money income or money turnover, is *stable*. This in turn implies that the velocity of circulation of money is stable, since the velocity of circulation is nothing else but the reciprocal of the demand for money expressed as a proportion of income or turnover – the two concepts are definitionally identical. Thus the quantity theory stands or falls with the proposition that the velocity of circulation of money is stable and invariant, or at least largely invariant, to changes in the quantity of money. If this were not so – if the velocity were a purely statistical relationship, as the Radcliffe Committee suggests, depending on what the relation of the quantity of money to the levels of incomes happened to be – there could be no direct or causal influence exerted by changes in the quantity of money on expenditure or on the level of prices.

'The supply of money' – whatever that may be made to mean – is not by itself a reliable policy measure, and the authorities must seek

[11] Ibid., para. 391.   [12] Ibid., para. 391.

rather to influence the general liquidity situation by operating on rates of interest. Given this approach regulation of the banks is required not because they are 'creators of money' but because they are the biggest lenders at the shortest (most liquid) end of the range of credit markets.

However, 'any severely restrictive control of these operations is certain, over a period of time, to be defeated by the development of rival institutions; during the interim, the community will have suffered loss by intereference with the most efficient channels of lending.'[13]

Before we end our consideration of the Radcliffe Committee's Report, something needs to be said of their notion of 'liquidity' or 'of the whole liquidity position' and how it contrasts with their notion of 'money'.

Unfortunately, neither concept is explicitly defined, though there are some hints that on any but the narrowest meaning of the term — i.e. *actual* means of payment — the concept of money is not really definable. Can the same thing be said of the wider notion of 'liquidity'? The same problem of where to draw the line appears, at first sight, to make it just as difficult to use the wider concept as the narrower one.

However, this need not be so. Liquid assets may be taken to refer to all such assets which can be exchanged for money (or for other liquid assets, normally through the intermediation of money), at any time, at short notice, and at a relatively small 'transaction cost' — meaning by this the difference between the net price at which the asset can be sold as against the net price at which it can be bought. The 'thicker' the market for an asset, and the more standardized the asset or commodity dealt with, the smaller the transaction cost will tend to be — ultimately it may disappear altogether.

This attribute is common to all those financial assets — or certificates of debt — the ownership of which is transferable: i.e., which are 'negotiable instruments' and which are freely and frequently trade in financial markets. The peculiarity of these assets is that they are held by their owners *both* as investment — that is to say, for their expected yield — *and* also as a store of potential purchasing power or spending power, which enables the owner to exploit an unforeseen opportunity to make a gain by converting them into money at short notice and at small cost, or else to use them as collateral for a loan. By contrast, *real* assets, such as land or houses, factories and machinery, furniture

---

[13] Ibid., para. 504.

and chattels, are *not* liquid assets. They are held by their owners for the direct benefits derived from their possession or for the expectation of a rise in their value (in the case of valuable paintings, for example) but they are not liquid assets because the owner can never be *certain* of being able to sell them at their 'true' value immediately — they are traded, if at all, in a 'thin' market where weeks or months may elapse before a suitable buyer can be found. There are, of course, real assets which have more of the attributes of 'liquid assets': gold or silver, for instance, whether minted into coins or held in the form of bars. Moreover, it is a universally accepted accounting convention to reckon as 'liquid assets' all those assets of a firm which are expected, in the normal course of business, to be sold for money in the near future, whether before or after they undergo transformation through processing or refinement or simply through breaking bulk.

Abstracting from these, however — and abstracting for the moment from a particular class of financial assets, the ordinary shares of publicly quoted companies — *all* financial assets are certificates of debt, repayable either on demand or at short notice, or after an interval of time measured in years or decades. The holders of such assets are therefore creditors, but the type of debt must be such as to create an asymmetrical situation between creditors and debtors — otherwise the asset of the creditor would be offset, from the point of view of liquidity, by the liability of the debtor. Loan transactions — borrowing and lending — *create* liquidity only when the claims of the creditors are more easily transferable from one person to another than the liabilites of the debtors. If I make a loan to a friend or neighbour, whether he gives me his personal IOU or not, *no* liquid asset is created. But if the same transaction takes place through financial intermediation — by my putting my current savings into a bank, and the bank making a loan to my neighbour — the general liquidity is increased since the addition of my claim on the bank increases the stock of liquid assets, whereas my neighbour does not regard his increased debt or overdraft as a corresponding reduction in *his* liquidity.

Thus private loan transactions give rise to additional liquidity if the process of lending and borrowing occurs, not directly, but through financial intermediaries. The best example is lending to a building society, which uses the money to grant mortgages to would-be houseowners that are repayable only over a large number of years. But the deposits which finance these mortgages are all repayable at short notice (a week or a month, and often without any prior notice whatsoever) because the societies know that while any particular depositor is able to withdraw his money immediately, there will be a sufficient accretion of new depositors to enable them to repay any particular depositor on demand and at the same time make long-term loans to borrowers.[14] It is all a matter of the building society setting the interest they pay at the right level in relation to other interest-paying financial institutions. There is no difference of any substance between the interest-paying deposit accounts of the clearing banks (which are officially reckoned as part of the 'money supply' on the broader definition, such as M3) and deposits with building societies, the magnitude of which, in Britain, is almost as large as that of the deposits of the clearing banks. The Government is in a peculiar position in that *all* of its debt consists of highly negotiable assets — with non-interest-paying bank notes at one end, through Treasury Bills, short bonds, medium- and long-dated bonds, down to perpetual bonds at the other end.[15] All are held in a dual capacity, as 'placements' or investments and also as sources of liquidity[16] — conferring the power on their owner to make sudden changes in the disposition of his wealth or to make investments financed by fresh borrowing.

Looked at in this way, there is no adequate reason for drawing a sharp line of distinction between bonds and shares — at least of those shares of major public companies which can be easily bought or sold in large amounts at a minute's notice. They both have the quality of easy 'transformability' — if I may use that ugly word — into other assets, and whether an individual holds the one or the other depends on his expectation of the net yield combined with the uncertainty of their future price. It is an aspect of the same 'portfolio decision' which causes an individual to distribute his wealth among financial assets of various types so as to maximize his 'net advantages' from owning wealth; the expected yield (including capital gains), flexibility, and marketability of the various types of financial assets all enter as elements in the notion of 'net advantages', though it would be misguided to carry too far the notion of 'rational choice' — the careful weighing of net advantages and their equalization at the margin — as against sheer ignorance or inertia.

---

[14] Something which could not be true if individuals with investible funds directly lent to their friends or others for house purchase secured by a mortgage.

[15] There are no 'perpetual bonds' in the literal meaning of the term. However, bonds such as Consols, which are repayable at any time at par at the Government's option, but the market value of which is much below par, are regarded in the same way as a perpetual annuity.

[16] In the case of 'cash' (money proper) the yield is a convenience yield.

The Radcliffe Committee maintained (and underlined through frequent repetition and emphasis) that the 'whole liquidity position' is relevant to spending decisions. In this they had in mind not only the greater readiness of individuals to spend on currently produced goods and services when they have a larger aggregate reserve of liquid assets, but also the fact that a large part of such assets are held by financial institutions — by banks, insurance companies, building societies, investment trusts, merchant banks, etc. — which means that the major effect of changes in interest rates is to be found 'in their repercussions on the behaviour of financial institutions'[17] rather than that of private individuals. 'The ease with which money can be raised depends on the one hand upon the composition of the spender's assets and on his borrowing power and on the other hand upon the methods, moods and resources of financial institutions, and other firms which are prepared (on terms) to finance other people's spending.'[18]

Given the fact that most, if not all, types of financial institutions have short-term liabilities, the interest payment on which varies in strict relation to the Bank Rate, whilst their assets consist in a large part of bonds or mortgages, the income from which is (or may be) fixed, there must clearly be limits to the freedom of the central bank to use the interest weapon if the solvency and viability of financial institutions is to be preserved. This is only one aspect of a wider problem of the Bank of England in its policies of debt-management (regarded by the Committee as the 'fundamental domestic task of the central bank'), which must be so conducted as to provide various types of debt in the amounts and proportions in which the public desires to hold them — subject to the Bank's powers to influence the public's preferences by altering the relative yield on various types of debt.

It is not open to the monetary authorities to be neutral in their handling of their task. They must have, and must consciously exercise, *a positive policy about interest rates*, long as well as short, and about the relationship between them.[19]

Unfortunately there is little in the Report that could serve as a guide to the Treasury or the Bank of England as regards such a positive policy, other than the somewhat cryptic statement that 'the authorities . . . should take a view as to what the *long term* economic situation demands and be prepared by all means in their power to influence markets in the required direction'.[20]

[17] Report, Cmnd. 827, para. 487.　　[18] Ibid., para. 389.
[19] Ibid., para. 982, italics added.　　[20] Ibid., para. 498, italics added.

If their recommendations had been fully adopted their effect would have been that the elasticity of substitution between different types of public sector debt would have become much greater, depending on the extent to which *relative* interest rates were held constant by the Bank's policies of debt-management. If in time the public came to believe that this policy would continue (as they did during the last war and the immediate post-war years) all Government debt would come to be regarded as equally liquid, since any one type could be exchanged for any other at stable conversion ratios.

As it is, a highly developed banking system already provides such facilities on an ample scale, since it is prepared to accommodate the public's changing demand between different types of financial assets by altering the composition of the banks' assets or liabilities in a reverse direction. If the non-banking public wishes to switch its holding of gilts for interest-bearing bank deposits, the banks are ready to supply such deposits at the minimum of inconvenience, and at the same time to place their surplus funds into the gilts which were previously held by the public. Similarly the banks provide easy facilities to their customers for switching balances on current accounts into interest-bearing deposit accounts, or vice versa. Hence, while the annual increment in the *total* holding of financial assets of the private sector (considered as a whole) is nothing more than the mirror-image of the borrowing requirement of the public sector (in a closed economy at any rate), neither the Government nor the banks can determine *how much* of this increment will be held in the form of cash (meaning notes and current deposits) and how much in the near-equivalents to cash (such as interest-bearing demand deposits) or in various forms of public sector debt. Thus neither the Government nor the central bank can *control* how much of the total financial assets the public prefers to hold in the form of 'money' on one particular definition or another.

All they can do is to vary the relative inducements of holding non-interest-bearing cash and interest-bearing deposits by varying the rate of interest, and as recent experience has shown, the effect of changes in the Minimum Lending Rate on the money stock as a proportion of incomes is quite insignificant in terms of the chosen target of the 'broad' definition of money, £M3. Clearly the public will tend to economize in cash (meaning notes and coins in circulation and non-interest-bearing current accounts) in response to a rise in the rate of interest paid on deposit accounts. Indeed the rise in the latter may exceed the fall in the former if the public wish to substitute interest-bearing deposits not only for 'money' in the narrow sense but also for the holding of bonds, the yield of which will not have risen as much as the interest on deposits. Thus between the last quarter of 1978 and the last quarter of 1980, the Minimum Lending Rate was raised twice, first to 14 per cent in June 1979 and then to 17 per cent in November; and in the following year it was reduced twice, first to 16 per cent in July 1980 and then to 14 per cent at the end of November. Over the two-year period GDP at current prices rose by 33 per cent while output prices rose by 36.25 per cent. But notes and coins in circulation rose by less than 17 per cent, non-interest-bearing current accounts by 11.8 per cent, and M1 (which is the sum of these two) rose by only 13.3 per cent. As against that, interest-bearing deposits rose by 58.6 per cent, and M3 (which is the sum of both types of deposits) by 32.8 per cent – at an almost identical rate as the money GDP.[21] The experience of these years thus gives ample proof of the inability of the authorities to prevent M3 from rising fully in line with the rise in incomes, despite the much-advertised 'tight money' policy which led to a fall in national output by 2.1 per cent and a fall in employment by 1.1 million, or 4.9 per cent of total employees in employment.

The only respect in which the Government have succeeded in their 'monetarist' policies is in reducing the increase in the 'money supply' in the *narrowest* sense of notes and coins in circulation plus non-interest bearing chequing accounts with the clearing banks (M1). This latter magnitude has in fact slowed down from a rise of 16.5 per cent in the

---

[21] It must be remembered that the concept of £M3 (the Government's chosen monetary target) only includes the savings deposits of the clearing banks, not the savings deposits held by building societies, trustee savings banks, etc. which make up 60 per cent of the total of interest-bearing deposits repayable at short notice. When these are included, the broadest measure of 'money' of the private sector (officially called PSL2) showed a rise of £27.8 billions over the same period, or an increase of 29.4 per cent – which is not much less than the 32.8 per cent shown by £M3. Moreover, the UK non-bank private sector took up £15.9 millions of public sector debt in these two years, which is not included in the concept of PSL2, so that the total increase in 'liquid assets' of the UK non-bank private sector *as a whole* (not including assets arising from lending to the private sector by the *non-bank* private sector) comes to £43.7 billions for the two years, or 35 per cent of the total of £124.7 billions outstanding at the end of 1978. (The total of £43.7 billions corresponds to the sum of two items: the cumulative PSBR for 1978-9 of £25.0 billions and the cumulative sterling lending by the banking sector to the UK non-bank private sector of £18.6 billions.) The above figures were derived from *Economic Trends*, November 1980, p. 90, Table 1, and *Financial Statistics* March 1981, Tables 7.3 and 7.6.

course of 1978, to only 9 per cent in 1979, and only 4 per cent in the course of 1980. But nobody wished to claim credit for that — not even the most monetarist of Ministers — since it was obvious to everybody that it was the result of a reduction of the public's demand for cash resulting from the high interest yield obtainable on other liquid securities; and the spectacular reduction in its rate of growth in no way signifies any 'downward pressure' on spending or on prices. In terms of wider concepts of liquidity, such as M3 or PSL2, the rate of increase was higher in the course of 1980 than in the previous year; and on the even broader notion of 'total liquidity', which the Radcliffe Report regarded as important, the rise in liquidity percentagewise was greater than the rise in the money value of the GNP, and this occurred at a time when the real economy plunged into deep recession. It could thus hardly be held responsible for an increase in the pressure of demand or an increase in 'spending decisions'.[22]

The recent revival of beliefs in the quantity theory of money — commonly called 'monetarism' — had its origin in empirical investigations purporting to show, in contrast to the views of the Radliffe Committee, the *stability* of the velocity of circulation. How this came about will be examined in the second of these lectures.

---

[22] It is significant that the only field in which the Radcliffe Committee detected an important reaction to credit control was in hire purchase credit — a type of lending for borrowers who possess little cash or liquid assets, and where the article sold — a car or a television set or furniture — itself provides the collateral for the loan. 'Tightening money' is only a powerful instrument in relation to the spending decisions of those people who possess little of it themselves.

LECTURE II

The main fault of the Radcliffe Report was that it interpreted its own terms of reference very narrowly, and having come to conclusions that were so largely negative, it did not attempt to give any outline, or even a hint, of its views of how the very real problems which monetary policy was called upon to deal with could be tackled. The Committee was undoubtedly well aware of these problems — not least because of the series of excellent memoranda which it received from distinguished British economists[1] — and these comprised the persistence of inflation and its world-wide character which was so contrary to previous experience; inadequate growth which they ascribed to insufficient long-term investment; inadequate export performance in relation to competitors; and cyclical instability leading at times to excessive pressure of demand.

Keynesian principles of economic management were universally accepted by all political parties and by academic economists — there were no monetarists of those days — and the question for discussion concerned only how the performance of the economy could be improved in terms of growth as well as the avoidance of inflation. The famous Coalition White Paper on Employment Policy of 1944 which accepted the maintenance of a high and stable level of employment as 'one of the Government's primary aims and responsibilities' was followed in 1956 by a further White Paper issued by a Conservative Government on the Economic Implications of Full Employment which stated that: 'The Government is pledged to foster conditions in which the nation can, if it so wills, realise its full potentialities for growth in terms of production and living standards'.[2]

The main instrument for attaining these ends was the regulation of the pressure of demand by fiscal policy supplemented by monetary policy, and the main question at issue was how the various objectives

---

[1] I can strongly recommend to present-day students the study of some of the memoranda reprinted in the third volume of the Committee's *Memoranda of Evidence*. The volume contains over thirty memoranda submitted by economists, a number of whom (particularly A. J. Brown, J. C. R. Dow, R. F. Harrod, R. F. Kahn, I. M. D. Little, R. R. Neild, and R. Ross) gave an excellent presentation of the issues that has lost none of its relevance — in sharp contrast with present-day writers on the subject, whose reasoning and terminology have been hopelessly befuddled by the outpourings of monetarist writers from across the Atlantic.

[2] Cmd. 9725, para. 25.

of policy − growth leading to rising living standards, as well as full employment, the avoidance of inflation, and a satisfactory balance of payments − could be pursued more successfully through a better orchestration of instruments.

The Keynesian model, on the basis of which economic management was conducted, had however one conspicuous weakness − it assumed money wages as exogenously given. Indeed, everything in the *General Theory* was measured in terms of 'wage units' − which meant that, in a closed economy, the rate of change in the price level was made to depend on the rate of increase in money wages relative to the rise in productivity. Fiscal and monetary policy were brought to bear to ensure the full utilization of resources but they were unavailing for dealing with wage-induced inflation. Some economists thought that keeping unemployment steady at a somewhat higher level − say 2.5 instead of 1.5 per cent − might suffice to prevent excessive wage increases; others, like myself, thought that full employment requires a permanent incomes policy, and elaborated a scheme to that effect as early as 1950. In fact a policy of restraint on personal incomes, introduced by Sir Stafford Cripps in 1948, successfully held the rise in wages and prices to below 3 per cent for two years in succession, 1949 and 1950, until the outbreak of the Korean war. But with the return of the Conservative Government in 1951, the political atmosphere for a scheme of this kind − which invariably involved the attainment of some consensus over the distribution of income between wages and profits − was lacking. So inflation went on − though in the second half of the 1950s, thanks to falling raw material prices, it did so at a lesser rate than before and almost came to a standstill in 1958-9. But in the 1960s it started up again, showing distinct signs of acceleration towards the end of that decade, probably as a result of the inflationary effects of the Vietnam war. The Committee with rare perspicacity concluded that '. . . the economy of the United Kingdom in the 1960s will, in the relevant ways, be more like that of the 1950s than like that of any earlier period.'[3]

Unbeknownst to the Committee a little man (I use this expression purely literally, meaning physical height, and in no other sense) was beavering away in America making correlations on times-series data which showed that fluctuations in the changes of the amount of money in circulation are closely related to changes in the level of aggregate

[3] Report of the *Committee on the Working of the Monetary System*, Cmnd. 827 (HMSO, August 1959), para. 86.

money income — the money national income. I am referring of course to Milton Friedman, who spent years in demonstrating a strong correlation between M and Y (where M stands for the stock of money and Y the money national income) and who convinced himself that this high correlation in itself constitutes a refutation of the Keynesian model of the economy and an empirical confirmation of the classical theory, the quantity theory of money.

The quantity theory of money which dominated both economic and political thought in the nineteenth century (the best proof of which was the Bank Charter Act of 1844) asserted that the value of money varies in inverse proportion to its quantity, the relationship depending on the demand to hold wealth in the form of money expressed as a proportion of income. Suppose people desire to hold a stock of money, or an average daily balance, which is the equivalent of three months' income on expenditure. Both Marshall and Walras asserted that since the *actual* size of balances are given exogenously by the quantity of gold in existence (they were postulating that gold was the money commodity), and since all the gold that is anywhere must be somewhere, there must be a mechanism to ensure that actual balances are brought into conformity with desired real balances, and that mechanism consists of changes in the value of gold in relation to other commodities. If actual balances exceed desired balances, and people increase their spending so as to get rid of the excess, the value of money will fall, and conversely. There is therefore a particular commodity value of gold which ensures conformity of actual with desired balances. This doctrine is not inconsistent with the proposition that the quantity of gold is only 'given' for the time being, and over a period it can be increased by new production or decreased by non-monetary uses of gold. In the long run, according to Ricardo and his followers, the value of gold will itself conform to its labour cost of production in the same way as in the case of other commodities.

There was, however, always a complication, due to the existence of paper money. Originally this was thought not to make any difference: paper money was preferred as more convenient to handle and to carry about, but it was really no more — or thought to be no more — than a cloakroom ticket for the gold deposited with trustworthy persons like goldsmiths, and, later, moneylenders or bankers, who had strong-rooms for safe keeping.

However, this simple idea about paper money could no longer be maintained when it was discovered, rather to the distaste of economists like Walras, that the volume of paper money in circulation was a multiple of the amount of gold deposited in the vaults of banks. But after further thought it was concluded that this does not make any difference either provided that paper money maintains its parity with gold through convertibility, and provided that there are firm rules or conventions, whether legal or prudential, to ensure convertibility. Still later this doctrine was extended when bank deposits became a further circulating medium, and then it was still further extended to the case of inconvertible paper currencies, provided that the quantity of paper money in circulation was determined quite exogenously by the fiat of the monetary authorities. After all, it was not the *intrinsic* value of gold but its limited quantity (its 'scarcity') which determined its value.

This was the dominant doctrine in which all Anglo-Saxon economists of the present century were brought up — whether Irving Fisher in America, or Keynes in Cambridge, who lectured on it for many years before and after World War I without questioning the basic principles. Its implications were that inflation is always the result of the 'over-issue' of banknotes (to use Ricardo's original expression), whether caused by the financial needs of Governments (as in times of war) or the greed of banks who (with the connivance of the Central Bank) extended too much bank credit.

Now Keynes's intellectual development, spread over several decades, consisted of a long struggle to escape from this theory; he succeeded in doing so in stages — which meant that he never abandoned it altogether.[4] The first stage was the realization that labour is different from commodities: the labour market is different from commodity markets, in that an excess supply will not cause a reduction in wages, nor does an excess demand necessarily lead to a rise in wages, at least not immediately. Hence his opposition to the return to the Gold Standard at pre-war parity: the domestic price level is tied to the level of wages which are not adjusted downwards so as to keep supply and demand in equilibrium.

The second stage came with the realization or recognition that effective demand for commodities in the aggregate is not determined by monetary factors but by autonomous demand financed by loan expenditures and the multiplier which depended on the propensity

---

[4] He himself complained, in an oft-quoted passage, of the difficulties of escaping from habitual modes of thought and expression, 'which ramify into every corner of our minds' (*The General Theory of Employment, Interest and Money* (London, 1936), Preface). Keynes was a pupil of Marshall and bore traces of it to the end of his life.

to save out of income. This meant that investment and savings, which are always brought into equality *ex post* do so through the adjustment of incomes and not, as the traditional theory had it, through movements in the rate of interest in the market for loans.

This left the rate of interest 'in the air', as Keynes himself put it (because it could no longer be held that the rate of interest is the 'price' which equates savings with investment), until he thought of the idea of liquidity preference — that people's demand for money will be the greater the lower the rate of interest — which provided the mechanism through which monetary variables accommodate themselves to the 'real factors', the underlying relationships which generate the equilibrium level of effective demand.

Unfortunately, the way he presented this solution was a *modification* of the quantity theory of money, not its *abandonment*. For he wrote:[5]

$$M = L(Y,r)$$

$$\text{or } M = k(r)\, Y$$

where $L(Y,r)$ represents the demand for money as a function of both the level of income Y and the rate of interest, r, while $k(r)$ represents the demand for money expressed as a *proportion* of income, and (according to Keynes) is an inverse function of the rate of interest. Or, to put the same thing in Fisher's terminology:

$$D \equiv Y = MV(r) \text{ (instead of } Y = MV)$$

This implies that *all* the adjustments of monetary to real factors are through changes in the velocity of circulation — since the quantity of money, M, is still shown as an independent variable, determined by the monetary authorities.

It was perhaps this form of presentation which led the Radcliffe Committee to the rather extreme-sounding statements about the variability of the velocity of circulation quoted in the first of these lectures. And it led young Milton Friedman into believing that the empirical validity of the Keynesian theory depended on the *absence* of any correlation between M and Y. Clearly if V adjusts to variations of Y, M and Y could not be closely related. Much to his surprise, he found the opposite — a strong correlation between M and Y. He worked and worked and re-worked the historical series on money and income on all the data he could get hold of, and then extended it in time, and though he encountered some difficulties he was able to eliminate these

[5] Ibid., p. 189.

by the postulate of a variable time-lag of a nature that changes in M always preceded changes in Y by anything between six months and two years. However, as even people with an elementary knowledge of statistics know, leads and lags can only be established at the turning-points of statistical series. Since in the time-series he examined (mainly data on money and income in the US) money and income were always rising (at least up to the Great Depression), sometimes faster and sometimes more slowly, it could not really be established whether either of the statistical series had a lead or a lag in relation to the other.

Moreover, Friedman's emphatic reassertion of the quantity theory of money — based on a stable *demand* function for money or a *stable* velocity: the two come to the same thing — was crucially dependent on the quantity of money being really exogenous, determined by the fiat of the monetary authorities quite independently of the demand for it. Or rather, in a dynamic context, it depended on the postulate that variations in the rate of increase in the money stock are the *cause* of variations in the rate of growth of money incomes occurring subsequently. When I first heard of Friedman's empirical findings, in the early 1950s, I received the news with some incredulity, until it suddenly dawned on me that Friedman's results must be read in *reverse*; the causation must run from Y to M, and not from M to Y. And the longer I thought about it the more convinced I became that a theory of the value of money based on a commodity-money economy it is not applicable to a credit-money economy. In the one case money has an independent supply function, based on production cost, while in the other case new money comes into existence in consequence of, or as an aspect of, the extension of bank credit. If, as a result, more money comes into existence than the public, at the given or expected level of incomes or expenditures, wishes to hold, the excess will be automatically *extinguished* — either through debt repayment or its conversion into interest-bearing assets — in a way in which gold could not be made to disappear from existence merely because particular persons find that they have too much of it. They can pass it on to others, but if they have less, others will have more. I find it difficult to get this point across except with the aid of a simple diagram. Keynes's theory of liquidity preference, as shown in that equation, has been diagrammatically represented in the following way:

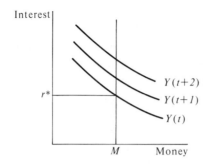

The supply of money is *given* as *M*, which is therefore a vertical line. The demand for money is the greater the lower the rate of interest, for any given level of *Y*. At a given *Y* there is a particular rate of interest, *r**, where the demand curve intersects the supply line — the rate of interest is therefore the 'price' which equates the demand and the supply of *money* (as a stock) — not the demand and supply for loans (which is a flow). The higher *Y* is, the higher is the demand for money — so with an increase in *Y* the curve is shifted to the right. A series of curves can be drawn for different levels of income and their point of intersection with *M*, the given money stock, can be represented as a *single LM curve* invented by Hicks, who represented Keynesian equilibrium at the point of intersection of an *IS* curve (the latter showing points of equality of savings and investment at different levels of income) with the *LM* curve. (This diagram became very popular, particularly in America, giving rise to endless complications and false conclusions, mainly because the two curves were not *in pari materia* — the one related to *stocks* and the other to *flows*.)

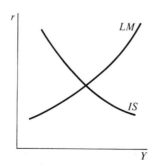

Now, in the case of credit money the proper representation should be a *horizontal* 'supply curve' of money not a vertical one. Monetary policy is represented *not* by a given quantity of money stock but by a *given rate of interest*; and the amount of money in existence will be demand-determined. Demand will vary with incomes as before, and it is possible that the rate of interest of the Central Bank (the old Bank Rate, now the MLR) will be varied upwards or downwards as a means of restricting credit or making credit easier, but this does not alter the fact that at any time, or at all times, the money stock will be determined by demand, and the rate of interest determined by the Central Bank.

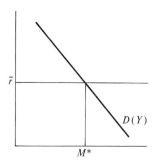

This means that from the point of view of that equation r is not a dependent but an independent variable; to determine r we need a further equation which in its simplest form could be written as:

$$r = \bar{r}$$

But of course from the point of view of any single country it could be a far more complicated equation, with the Bank Rate or Minimum Lending Rate being a function of the level, or of the rate of change in Central Bank reserves, of gold or foreign currencies, and/or the rate of interest in other financial centres, etc. To the extent that Friedman is right in his empirical conclusion that the demand for money, or rather the velocity of circulation, is not sensitive to changes in the rate of interest, the money stock becomes mainly dependent on demand, governed by the level of incomes; and monetary policy based on interest rate changes is totally ineffective as a regulator of the money *supply*. Any effect is thus an indirect one via the influence of changes in the interest rate on investment and hence on the level of incomes generated by a Keynesian multiplier-accelerator process. It is an influence on the demand for money exerted through changes in the level of production and incomes, and not a *direct* effect on the desire to hold money.

Whilst monetarists continually emphasize that the Central Bank can or should directly determine the *quantity of money*, or at least the 'base stock' of money, consisting of banknotes and bankers' reserves (or balances) with the Central Bank, in fact they can do no such thing, as a recent experience with the Federal Reserve or the Bank of England shows. (Even Friedman admitted this recently when he said that incompetent Central Banks like the Bank of England are not *capable* of regulating the money supply.) They cannot prevent either a depletion or an accumulation of 'high powered money' (or reserve money) except by a policy of en- or discouragement — by raising or lowering the rate at which they are prepared to create reserves by discounting (or re-discounting) Treasury Bills and bonds. But the Central Bank cannot close the 'discount window' without endangering the solvency of the banking system; they must maintain their function as a 'lender of last resort'. Equally they cannot prevent any depletion of Government balances with the Bank of England due to an excess of outgo over inflow from reappearing as an *addition* to high powered bank money — not unless they refuse to honour cheques issued by HMG — which would be a rather drastic step for monetarists to take.

The present directors of the Federal Reserve and of the US Treasury are all-out monetarists. But this does not make them capable of determining what the quantity of money on any particular definition should be on a particular day or week or month — all they can do is to raise or lower the discount rates when the growth of money stock runs ahead of, or behind, the target. The Radcliffe Committee understood this well, though they have not succeeded in explaining it very well. Anyhow, they insisted that the primary function of the Central Bank is to determine interest rates, and *not* the quantity of money; which is a view consistent with my diagrammatic representation of the supply-of-money function.

Friedman's empirical findings were originally directed to prove that the money has a *stable demand function* which does not respond at all, or responds very little, to changes in the rate of interest. Clearly, if you have a broad definition of money which includes interest-bearing deposits, there is no reason why the *demand* for money should respond at all to changes in the rate of interest at a given level of incomes. The demand curve could be vertical or even positively sloping — as we have seen was the case with M3 during the period of the present Government. 'Liquidity preference' turns out to have been a bit of a red herring – not the 'crucial factor' which, in the view of the great economists of Keynes's generation, such as Dennis Robertson or Jacob Viner, and, of a later generation, Harry Johnson or James Tobin, alone enabled Keynes to argue that an economy can be in equilibrium at less than full employment. It has nothing to do with that at all.

Friedman, to his credit, admitted that his whole position depends entirely on the causative chain running from money to income and not the other way round, and while conceding that the question of the direction of causality is not finally settled, he gave various reasons for preferring his way of looking at it. These 'reasons' gave rise to endless debates in the US, and none of them, in the end, proved water-tight – none of them really served to buttress his case. In response to an article of mine in which I attacked the new gospel in a rather humorous vein in 1970, Friedman wrote a somewhat ill-tempered reply[6] which ended with the following paragraph:

The reader can judge the weight of the casual empirical evidence for Britain since the Second World War that Professor Kaldor offers in rebuttal by asking himself how Professor Kaldor would explain the existence of essentially the same relation between money and income for the U.K. after the Second World War as before the First World War, for the U.K. as for the U.S., Yugoslavia, Greece, Israel, India, Japan, Korea, Chile and Brazil? If the relation between money and income is a supply response, as Professor Kaldor asserts that it is for the U.K. since the Second World War, how is it that major differences among countries and periods in monetary institutions and other factors affecting the supply of money do not produce widely different relations between money and income?

The simple answer to this is that Friedman's assertions lack any factual foundation whatsoever. They have no basis in fact, and he seems to me to have invented them on the spur of the moment. I had the relevant figures extracted from IMF statistics for 1958 and for each of the years 1968 to 1979, for every country mentioned by Friedman and a few others besides. The tables containing these data can be found in the Annexe to this lecture. Though there are some countries (among which the US is conspicuous) where in terms of M3 the ratio has been fairly stable over the period of observation, this was not true of the

[6] See Annexe to this lecture.

majority of others, and the ratio also shows the widest possible differences between countries as well as between periods, both on the broad definition (M3) and the narrow definition (M1). Thus in 1978, the ratio of money (M3) to income was as much as 125.6 per cent in Switzerland, 96.5 per cent in Italy, 83 per cent in Israel, 87.2 per cent in Japan, but only 34.3 per cent in the UK, 33.8 per cent in Korea, and only around 15 per cent in Chile and Brazil.[7] Going further back in history, in the UK it held fairly steady at between 55 and 60 per cent during the cheap money era of the 1930s, and then rose during and after the war to reach its peak at 80 per cent in 1948, thereafter falling steadily down to 44 per cent in 1958 and (ignoring the Heath period) to 34.3 per cent in 1978. In the case of Germany, the ratio was as little as one-half of 1 per cent in the latter phase of the Great Inflation of 1923; in post-World War II Germany it started at 10 to 15 per cent after the monetary reform and then rose pretty steadily to 36 per cent by 1958, 52 per cent by 1968, and 56.8 per cent by 1978. In other words it is in the country with the *lowest* inflation rate that the money supply has shown a persistent rate of growth in excess of the rise in money income — something which on Friedman's principles is bound to lead to inflation, with a two year lag. In Germany, however, it failed to do so with a twenty year lag. Again, in Chile, where the Government indulged in the most unsound finance during the Allende years, spending like mad without raising taxes, the ratio of money supply to the money income *rose* from 18 per cent to 40 per cent in the period 1970-3, and later, when Friedman became economic or monetary adviser to Pinochet, the ratio *fell* from 40 per cent to 14.7 per cent — in other words the velocity of circulation fell substantially during the years of easy money, and rose very substantially during the years of strict monetarism — the opposite of what one would expect if the inflation had monetary causes, and quite incompatible in any case with any hypothesis of 'rational expectations'.

But even if Friedman had been right about the stability and uniformity in the *demand* for money, it would not have been really relevant to the issue whether the *supply* of money is exogenous or endogenous. It is quite possible (though highly unlikely) for all economic agents, and all national economies, to show the same *demand* for money and yet for the stock of money to vary automatically in

[7] The figures for Chile and Brazil are approximate. All other figures (except for Italy) are given in Table II of the Annexe to this lecture.

response to variations in demand: i.e. for the money stock to be demand-determined, and not supply-determined. Indeed, for reasons I have given, this is *more likely* to be so the less the demand for money varies with the rate of interest — a stable velocity in response to interest rate variations is evidence, not of the importance or potential importance of monetary controls, but of their *impotence*.

But of course there were other difficulties in the Friedman view of causation. The normal method of Central Banks if they wish to stimulate the economy is to reduce the rate of interest, and to make this effective by open market operations in the money market. They can thereby keep the rate of interest on the market at the desired level (which is always somewhat below their own rate of re-discount) by buying bills from the market to bring the rate down, or by selling bills in order to raise the rate. But from then on the reaction of the *real* economy to such changes will depend on a purely Keynesian mechanism — the response of stock-building or house-building, and possibly other forms of investment, to a lower rate of interest, and the response of personal consumption out of a given income (or on the propensity to save, which is the same thing) to the lower interest rate. All empirical enquiries relating to Britain — such as the famous Hall-Hitch enquiry before the War, and the enquiries of the Radcliffe Committee — came to the conclusion that apart from hire purchase and housebuilding, changes in interest rates within the range of variations actually experienced have very little effect on either capital expenditures or consumption expenditures — certainly not the proportionate effect postulated by the monetarists.

This, according to Friedman, is only because the effect is always delayed by two years and hence not immediately discernible. But why should it be delayed? and what happens in between? The transmission mechanism from money to income remained a 'black box' — he could not explain it, and he did not attempt to explain it either. When it came to the question of *how* the authorities increase the supply of bank notes in circulation he answered that they are scattered over populated areas by means of a helicopter — though he did not go into the ultimate consequences of such an aerial Santa Claus. If the money were scattered over a poor area, like the East End of London, most of the people who picked it up, whether adults or children, would be full of unsatisfied desires, and perhaps empty stomachs, so they could be expected to spend it. If it were scattered in a wealthy area, like Kensington Palace Gardens, most of the money would be picked up by servants and gardeners and handed over in all honesty to their masters who would add it to their bank accounts – unless they gave the money to a charity. So the 'first-round effects' of the helicopter operation could be anything, depending on where the scatter occurred. However, the *subsequent effects* would be quite insignificant – unless the operation was repeated night after night. For a once-and-for-all effect on spending, even though it would be quite large in terms of daily expenditure, it might be insignificant in terms of annual expenditures, and there is no reason for supposing that its effect on incomes, let alone prices, would be proportionate to the amount of money scattered in relation to the pre-existing money stocks. For whether the money were spent or not by its initial recipients, it would be bound to be largely returned to the banks by the second recipients (the traders who sold the goods on which the money was spent) and there is no reason to suppose that the ultimate effect on the amount of money in circulation or on the level of incomes would bear any close relation to the initial injection.

Moreover, there was other evidence that the 'stability of velocity' – or rather its invariance with respect to changes in the money stock – on which the theory so critically depended was not a firm feature at all: it was a mirage. The Radcliffe Committee were right to emphasize that velocity can vary within very wide limits, and if it does not, it is only because the ease of response of the money supply to changes in the volume of money transactions makes changes in velocity superfluous. When the response of the money supply is not complete – in other words when the money stock does not rise fully in proportion to the rise in expenditures – the velocity of circulation rises to make up the difference; in the opposite case it slows down. In other words, changes in the stock of money and changes in velocity are substitutes to one another; if the velocity of circulation *appears* stable it is only because the quantity of the money stock is so *unstable*.[8]

These shortcomings, and the increasing doubts about the postulate of causation in the relationship of money to money income, must have stimulated the emergence of a new version of monetarism: Monetarism Mark II, as Professor Tobin called it. It is represented by a new generation of American economists – names like Barro, Lucas, Sargent, Mayer – and a few British ones, such as Professor Patrick Minford.

[8] The clearest historical example is the experience of the US and Canada during the Great Depression, 1929–32. The *money* GNP fell at an almost identical rate in the two countries, but because there were no bank failures in Canada, the fall in the 'money supply' there was considerably smaller, and the fall in the velocity of circulation correspondingly *larger*.

As far as I understand it, they accept the Keynesian reaction mechanism as to how money *gets into circulation*, but assert that inflation is invariably due to excess spending at a national level which in turn is caused by the Government spending too much or at least too much in relation to their tax revenue (that is, borrowing too much), and if the appearances belie this — for example, when it occurs in a period of falling output and rising unemployment — it is only because 'economic agents' (in other words the 'man in the street') unlike Ministers or Civil Servants, economic forecasters or Stock Exchange speculators, have *rational expectations*: a thinly-disguised name for perfect foresight. They can tell what is going to happen, simply because it is in their interest to know. The great advantage of Monetarism Mark II over Mark I is that its protagonists need not attempt to justify their theories by empirical tests — though they use econometric models in plenty, these serve to quantify predictions (of the type that 'a 1 per cent rise in unemployment lowers the inflation rate *ultimately* by 5 per cent') *given* the specifications of their model, but not to test the specification itself. Indeed, they could hardly be asked to do the latter since the behavioural equations depend so largely on expectations concerning the future, and expectations and their changes have the peculiar property that they cannot be empirically *observed*, which puts their models beyond the realm where they can be refuted. Whatever happens, you can always infer some set of expectations (or better, some set of *changes* in expectations) which explain observed events within the framework of the model. It is a basic principle of the Chicago School of positive economics that the assumptions (or postulates) on which an economic model is based need not in themselves be based on empirical observation; they can be quite unrealistic provided that they perform well; and since performance can only be judged in relation to past events, while the assumptions are no more capable of empirical confirmation *ex post facto* than *ex ante*, 'good performance' amounts to no more than the vacuous proposition that the state of expectations at time T must have been such as to produce the events which actually occurred at times $T+1$ — thereby both 'explaining' what occurred and confirming the assumption of rational expectations at the same time.

Professor Hahn, in a recent article in *The Times* on the 'Preposterous Claims of the Monetarists',[9] has done a great service by listing some of the assumptions on which Monetarism Mark II is based. There is

9 *The Times*, 28 April 1981, p. 19.

universal perfect competition – each producer or seller can sell indefinite amounts at the ruling market price; all markets continually
'clear', which means that they are *always* in equilibrium; there can
never be any excess supply or demand due to insufficient price adjustment hence production is *always* supply-constrained even when manufacturers and traders complain of lack of orders and are dismissing
workers wholesale because there is no work for them. I suppose the
monetarists would concede this to the extent of saying that owing
to some change in expectations the workers are not 'wanted' at the
existing or expected level of real wages. But – according to their
argument – there is *always* a real wage or an expected real wage at
which jobs can be found for everybody at any time, so if people are
nevertheless unemployed it is only because they prefer 'to substitute
present for future leisure', or because the difference between the wage
they could get now and unemployment benefit which they get when
they are not working is insufficient to compensate them for the disutility
of labour (although this does not answer the question of why unemployment has been so low in the past when the compensation for the
disutility of labour was just as small as it is today). Hence all employment is *voluntary*; any stimulation of demand therefore would not
increase output but simply increase the rate of inflation; economic
policy should therefore aim to improve the 'supply side' of the economy
by giving better incentives to work and greater disincentives for *not*
working, and thereby increase production which is never limited by
lack of demand. This is all the more necessary because economic agents
(including, I presume, collective agents like trade unions) have a correct
perception of how the economy works, and therefore any change in
the Government borrowing, or in the money stock associated with
greater spending, leads them to anticipate that prices will rise in the
same proportion as the money stock, and therefore to adjust their
behaviour immediately to it – raising wages in proportion if there is
a rise in the money stock, and reducing wages with equal ease when
the money stock falls. Hence, again, all unemployment is always voluntary, not involuntary.

The dilemma of Mark II Monetarism, as Professor Tobin pointed
out,[10] is that it is compelled to regard inflation as quite harmless and
as a great evil at the same time – two views which are not easy to
reconcile with one another. If all price increases are always fully antici-
pated and everybody performs the same way whether there is inflation

----

[10] *Economic Journal*, March 1981, p. 35.

or not, then why does inflation matter? The only *real* cost of inflation, according to Monetarism Mark II, is the increased real cost of holding money and the inconvenience involved in holding less — which is admitted to be a small loss. Why should it be regarded as the first priority to get rid of it, overriding all other objectives? The answer follows from Mrs Thatcher's own view, apparently shared by some of her Ministers, that in a non-inflationary economy everybody would work harder and more efficiently. Unfortunately this latter view (whether true or not) finds no support in the theoretical doctrines from which she claims to have derived her views.

But nor does the large fall in output and employment which has occurred in the last two years, despite an accelerated growth in the money supply, M3, in the PSBR as a percentage of the GDP, and in over-all liquidity. Why should an *unsuccessful* attempt to reduce the PSBR and to slow down the growth of the money stock result in a deep economic depression? According to the figures churned out by the Central Statistical Office, the fall in output was due, not to reduced exports (for that was more than offset by the fall in imports), nor to reduced private consumption (because *in toto* real personal consumption had not fallen), nor to reduced Government consumption (because that had risen), nor to lower fixed capital formation (because its fall in real terms was relatively modest — some £400m. in 1975 prices), but almost exclusively to an enormous swing in stock-building which, in terms of 1975 prices, showed a turn-round of nearly £3.5 billions (from +£1.6 billion in 1979 to —£1.8 billion in 1980), and which in turn was not a result of the credit squeeze — because though interest rates were higher there was no real credit squeeze such as in 1974-5, as the current banking figures show. It must therefore have reflected the emergence of highly pessimistic expectations by firms concerning future sales, due to their belief in the firmness of the Government's deflationary goals, and the announcement of the Government's medium-term strategy, as well as the over-valuation of the pound which generated a squeeze on profits. And since orders *did* fall off, these expectations were not irrational — it was a self-fulfilling prophecy, even if things did not run out quite the same way the Government's announced medium-term strategy proclaimed.

ANNEXE

Extract from a Comment by Professor Milton Friedman[11] *in Response to an Article by Nicholas Kaldor on 'The New Monetarism'.*[12]

In the article he contributed to the July issue of this *Review*, Professor Kaldor makes one central point: that changes in the money supply must be regarded as the result, not the cause, of changes in economic activity. He states this point in different ways, embellishing it with assorted illustrations, each time as if it were a profound idea that had never occurred to the well-meaning but benighted monetarists he is attacking. Strip this point from his discussion and there remains mostly rhetoric — some of it clever, some of it accurate, much of it neither. Establish this point, and his case against monetarists is firm: pins move with the cycle; money moves with the cycle; this is evidence of neither a pin theory of the cycle nor a monetary theory of the cycle but of the pervasive influence of cyclical fluctuations.

As it happens Professor Kaldor is a Johnny-come-lately with this point. The monetarists themselves recognised its importance from the outset, and, if they had not, their U.S. critics have for the past decade repeatedly flourished it. . . .

As a result, this issue has been explored intensively. The outcome is about as decisive as the answer to any such question can ever be: clearly, there are influences running from income to the quantity of money, as Professor Kaldor asserts but, equally clearly, there are strong influences running from the quantity of money to income. The latter do not and should not exclude the former.

I have summarised the evidence for the influence of money in an article reprinted in a book to which Professor Kaldor refers, but which he apparently has not read . . .[13]

After summarising the evidence under . . . five headings, I concluded:

> In a scientific problem, the final verdict is never in. Any conclusion must always be subject to revision in the light of new evidence. Yet I believe that the available evidence of the five kinds listed justifies considerable confidence in the conclusion that the money series is dominated by positive conformity, which

[11] *Lloyd's Bank Review*, October 1970.
[12] *Lloyd's Bank Review*, July 1970.
[13] 'The Monetary Studies of the National Bureau' (National Bureau of Economic Research, 44th Annual Report, New York, 1964, pp. 7–25), reprinted in *The Optimum Quantity of Money and Other Essays* (London, 1969), pp. 266–84.

reflects in some measure an independent influence of money on business. The feedback effect of business on money, which undoubtedly also exists, may contribute to the positive conformity and may also introduce a measure of inverted conformity.

The reader can judge the weight of the casual empirical evidence for Britain since the Second World War that Professor Kaldor offers in rebuttal by asking himself how Professor Kaldor would explain the existence of essentially the same relation between money and income for the U.K. after the Second World War as before the First World War, for the U.K. as for the U.S., Yugoslavia, Greece, Israel, India, Japan, Korea, Chile and Brazil? If the relation between money and income is a supply response, as Professor Kaldor asserts that it is for the U.K. since the Second World War, how is it that major differences among countries and periods in monetary institutions and other factors affecting the supply of money do not produce widely different relations between money and income?

TABLE I

Ratio of Narrow Money Supply (M1) to GNP (in percentages)[1]

	1958	1968	1969	1970	1971	1972	1973	1974	1975	1976	1977	1978	1979
UK	n/a	20.1	18.8	18.7	19.2	19.9	18.0	17.5	16.6	15.5	16.5	16.7	15.8
US	31.6	24.1	23.1	23.0	22.6	22.4	21.3	19.9	19.3	18.4	17.9	17.1	16.1
Yugoslavia	n/a	24.1	23.1	22.7	20.8	24.6	27.3	26.4	27.6	36.2	34.3	34.4	n/a
Greece	12.9	19.4	18.0	17.9	18.8	19.6	18.8	19.3	18.9	18.8	18.8	19.1	18.0
Israel	18.8	21.1	18.7	18.3	18.7	18.8	19.8	16.5	14.2	13.9	13.3	11.9	8.2
India	n/a	16.3	16.5	16.9	17.8	18.2	17.3	16.1	16.8	19.9	20.1	22.6	n/a
Japan	22.6	28.8	29.7	29.1	34.2	37.2	35.6	33.3	33.6	33.6	32.6	33.6	32.1
Korea	11.4	11.1	12.1	11.5	10.9	13.0	14.0	12.9	12.1	11.6	12.8	11.8	11.3
Chile	7.6	11.1	9.2	10.5	17.3	22.7	18.7	8.8	7.4	6.2	5.8	n/a	n/a
Brazil	23.5	17.5	17.1	16.8	16.4	17.5	19.0	17.6	17.5	15.7	14.5	13.7	14.2
France	31.2	34.0	28.4	29.5	29.5	30.3	29.2	29.4	29.2	27.1	26.9	26.4	25.8
Germany	17.1	16.5	15.7	15.1	15.3	15.9	14.4	15.5	16.8	15.9	16.8	17.8	16.7
Switzerland	52.9	47.8	49.0	48.7	50.5	47.0	42.1	37.1	39.3	42.7	41.7	48.0	45.4

[1] The countries chosen were those mentioned by Milton Friedman as having 'essentially the same relation between money and income' both in different periods and in relation to each other. The last three countries were added for the sake of comparison.

Source: IMF International Financial Statistics, April 1981 and earlier issues.

TABLE II
Ratio of Broad Money Supply (M3) to GNP (in percentages)[1]

	1958	1968	1969	1970	1971	1972	1973	1974	1975	1976	1977	1978	1979
UK	40.6	36.4	35.0	34.8	35.3	40.8	44.8	44.4	38.1	35.6	34.3	34.2	33.3
US	45.5	46.7	43.0	45.9	47.7	48.7	48.5	48.0	47.2	46.0	45.4	44.5	42.7
Yugoslavia	n/a	63.2	64.2	65.9	63.5	65.4	69.2	65.9	69.1	78.1	78.3	84.3	n/a
Greece	25.5	47.3	48.3	51.2	56.2	60.4	54.5	55.8	58.7	59.4	63.4	64.4	61.1
Israel	25.6	50.6	50.7	52.2	55.5	55.2	54.9	59.1	55.3	62.4	79.7	83.0	90.6
India	n/a	23.8	24.4	25.3	27.4	28.7	27.7	26.2	28.4	33.4	34.5	38.7	n/a
Japan	49.6	74.4	75.3	73.8	83.3	90.6	86.8	81.1	84.2	85.0	84.9	87.2	87.4
Korea	12.7	27.3	33.9	33.6	33.1	36.3	38.0	33.2	31.8	31.1	33.8	33.8	34.0
Chile	9.4	17.8	16.9	17.9	26.8	35.3	40.0	22.1	18.4	14.0	14.7	n/a	n/a
Brazil	25.7	19.8	19.8	19.7	18.7	19.3	20.6	19.0	19.1	17.0	16.4	16.4	17.0
France	33.4	45.3	40.7	43.7	46.3	49.0	49.5	50.9	52.0	50.5	51.6	51.1	50.9
Germany	36.0	53.2	53.1	52.0	53.8	56.7	56.8	51.0	54.2	53.6	55.5	56.8	54.8
Switzerland	98.5	106.5	116.7	118.6	114.7	109.5	103.3	98.7	108.2	114.6	117.6	125.6	133.3

[1] See footnote to Table I above.

Source: IMF International Financial Statistics, April 1981 and earlier issues.

PART II

Monetary Policy in the United Kingdom

TABLE OF CONTENTS

EVIDENCE TO THE TREASURY AND CIVIL SERVICE COMMITTEE JULY 1980[1]

I. INTRODUCTION

1. I was requested to submit evidence to the Treasury and Civil Service Committee for purposes of their inquiry into monetary policy, and for this purpose was sent a detailed questionnaire comprising thirty-five questions classified under three heads (excluding questions in the Appendix). I found after consideration that any attempt to answer the questions individually (whether comprehensively or selectively) would make it very difficult to present my views in a coherent manner. I therefore prefer to give my views in the form of a memorandum divided into sections followed by brief comments on a number of particular issues raised in the Committee's questionnaire.

2. I should like, however, by way of introduction to give an explicit answer to the first question. I believe that the four objectives listed there ((a) full and stable employment, (b) a satisfactory balance of payments, (c) the absence of inflation, (d) a high rate of economic growth) should severally and jointly, be regarded as the *main* objectives of Governmental 'economic management'. In that respect my views have not changed (or at least not significantly) since my address to the British Association in 1970.[2] I believed then, and I believe now, that the simultaneous pursuit of these objectives requires a multiplicity of instruments (ideally the same number as there are objectives) though a given policy measure might have a favourable effect on the attainment of several objectives simultaneously, or else have a favourable effect on some and an unfavourable effect on others. In general it has been supposed that higher priority given to (*a*) and (*d*) is likely to be at the cost of (*b*) and (*c*) — i.e. policies aimed at a higher level of employment and of economic growth may have adverse effects on the balance of payments and on inflation. But this is not invariably true. For example a *successful* policy aiming at export-led growth may lead to a higher

---

[1] I am indebted to Mr Paul Atkinson, Mr Ken Coutts, and Miss Margaret Clark of the Department of Applied Economics, Cambridge, for assistance in the preparation of the tables, and to the Controller of HMSO for permission to reprint.

[2] 'Conflicts in National Economic Objectives', *Economic Journal*, March 1971.

rate of growth of manufacturing industry and thereby a higher rate of growth of productivity in the economy generally; it may at the same time improve the balance of payments and lower the rate of inflation both through its effect on the exchange rate and import prices, and also through the effects of a higher rate of growth of disposable real incomes on wage demands. But a policy of this kind may require different instruments, or different ways of operating conventional instruments, from those that were customary during the post-war (full employment) period.

3. In so far as there is a conflict between the simultaneous pursuit of objectives, I think policies which strengthen the 'real' economy — i.e. output, employment, capital formation, and the rate of economic growth — ought to be given higher weight than 'monetary objectives', such as a lower rate of inflation and a stronger balance of payments. I am sceptical, however, of econometric models which aim at discovering an 'optimal policy mix' on the basis of a particular 'model' of the workings of the economy, the predictions of which depend critically on the period of history observed, the variables chosen, and the manner in which the empirical values of the coefficients are estimated. While economic models may be helpful in the utilization of statistical material for forecasting purposes, in the last resort the 'best' combination of policies must remain a matter of flair and insight, not susceptible to precise calculation.

4. The main shortcoming of post-war 'full employment' policies (in the British context) was that they regarded the problem of insufficient demand as if it had been mainly due to insufficient investment in relation to the amount of savings forthcoming at full employment, rather than of insufficient exports in relation to imports associated with full-employment income. Hence the policy instruments were designed to generate 'consumption-led' growth rather than 'export-led' growth which, by its very nature, militated against a fast growth of productivity and involved policy-generated instabilities in reaction to periodic balance-of-payments crises.

5. I regard the present Government's view of giving 'over-riding priority to reducing inflation' as a thoroughly mistaken one (a) because reducing inflation should not have 'over-riding priority' at the cost of sacrificing all other objectives; (b) the instruments adopted are ill-fitted to produce the intended results — indeed they may serve to aggravate inflation instead of reducing it; (c) because it is a policy pursued which damages the 'supply side of the economy' by lowering output, employment, and productivity, and, still more important, by

lowering capital investment. These unfavourable effects are not self-reversing but on the contrary are self-reinforcing.

6. The Government's current economic policies are justified by reference to the basic tenets of monetarism. In the following sections I consider (i) what are the main claims of the monetarists; (ii) what particular set of assumptions concerning the workings of the economy are necessary for those claims to be valid; (iii) what are the critical ways in which an economic system in reality differs from that assumed by the monetarists; (iv) how the policies and pronouncements of the Government depart from pure monetarist doctrine and the implications of those departures.

II. THE BASIC POSTULATES OF 'MONETARISM' AND THEIR IMPLICATIONS

7. The main propositions of monetarism are (i) that the rate of increase in the money supply (in excess of the rate warranted by the growth in real output) is the main determinant, if not the sole cause, of the rate of increase in the prices of goods and services; (ii) that apart from short-term disturbances caused by the failure to foresee the future correctly (irrational expectations) the movement of the 'real economy' — i.e. output, employment, and productivity growth — are fully determined by 'real factors' such as technical progress, the growth in effective labour supply, and the rate of capital formation — all of which are determined by market forces independently of changes in the money supply except for temporary disturbances (which may be positive or negative in terms of real output or employment), due to imperfect foresight. In the 'long run', however, real output and its distribution are fully determined by such 'real' factors; there is no scope for any macro-policies with the objectives listed above except for the control of inflation which can be achieved (and only achieved) by control of the money supply.

8. Before we commence to examine the assumptions behind these views, a number of questions present themselves:

(i) Assuming that the behaviour of the 'real' economy is neutral with respect to monetary disturbances, why should the elimination of inflation be such an important objective as to be given 'over-riding priority'? In what way is a community better off with constant prices than with constantly rising (or falling) prices? The answer evidently must be that, in the view of the Government, inflation causes serious distortions and leads to a deterioration in economic performance, etc. In that case, however, the basic proposition that the 'real' economy is impervious to such disturbances in untenable.[3]

(ii) If the rise in prices is a direct consequence of the increase in the supply of money – whether that which takes place currently or that which took place some years back – why allow any further increase in the supply of money to take place at all? (According to Table 5 of the Red Book (issued annually with the Budget) the target for the growth of the money supply is a very gradual fall over the next few years, and even in 1983–4 it is considerably in excess of the postulated growth in real GNP.) If, as the Government proclaim, the elimination of inflation is a pre-condition for the resumption of sound growth, why not get inflation over as quickly as possible, instead of spreading it over a number of years; and if the latter, why did they allow the rate of inflation to double in the first year in office thereby making the task that much greater – was it just *reculer pour mieux sauter*? If the Government's answer is that it is impossible to telescope the process into a shorter period – by keeping the money supply constant or even decreasing it for some time – the Government should be asked just what the obstacle is. (One frequently mentioned obstacle, 'inflationary expectations', will be discussed later.)

III. THE MODEL OF THE ECONOMY UNDERLYING THE MONETARIST VIEW

9. The monetarist propositions could be applied to an imaginary economy, such as it postulated in Walras's famous model of general equilibrium.[4] This assumes that there are a finite number of 'commodities' (both products and 'services'[5]) which are traded in perfect markets, under conditions of perfect competition where one of the commodities serves as money (normally a precious metal like gold or silver); its

[3] It would however be advisable for the Committee to asertain from Ministers the nature of the ill-effects associated with inflation, and to quantify them if possible.

[4] In *Elements of Pure Economics* (1st ed. Lausanne, 1874, final def. ed. 1926); English translation by W. Jaffé (London, 1954).

[5] By which latter he meant the hire-price of the services of the factors of production, i.e. the wages of labour as well as the rent of land, etc.

use as money creates added demand for it because both producers and consumers desire to maintain a certain cash balance in relation to their income (i.e. in their command over commodities in general).[6] Since in a perfect market every commodity (including money) must settle at its 'market-clearing' price, where demand and supply are equal (in the sense that there are no unsatisfied buyers or sellers) and a rise in the price of a commodity could only occur as a result of an excess demand, and correspondingly, a fall in the price of the money-commodity signifies an excess supply of that commodity which comes to the same thing (under these assumptions) as an excess demand for *all* other commodities. In equilibrium the *value* of money will settle at the point where it no longer exceeds, or falls short of, the desired cash balances of all participants. The peculiarity of the demand for the money-commodity (as against other commodities) is that its 'marginal utility' varies in strict inverse proportion to its quantity, so that the value of the total cash balance in terms of other commodities is invariant to changes in the quantity of the money-commodity available for monetary use. (This of course is the assumption underlying the quantity theory of money.) A falling trend in the value of the money-commodity arises when the supply of the money-commodity increases faster than the supply of all other commodities taken together; this may happen as a result of the discovery of new gold or silver mines, or the invention of 'substitutes' for the money-commodity in the form of (circulating) bank notes and cheques which enable the total money supply to

[6] It is not clear from Walras's account just what the function of money is under the highly abstract assumptions of static general equilibrium. One set of the equations which determines that equilibrium is that each individual 'transactor' satisfies his own 'budget equation', i.e. the value of his purchases of goods and services is equal to the value of his sales of goods and services at the same point of time or over the same period so that when both are measured in terms of a common unit, the numeraire, receipts and payments can be cleared by a system of mutual 'offsets' (a kind of giro) without the intermediary of money. The numeraire must exist, but the numeraire is a commodity (it could be wheat or oxen) which serves as a unit of account, not money in the sense of a medium of exchange or a store of general purchasing power. Money is required, as Walras says in § 273, when services have to be paid for at one *fixed* date and payments have to be made for the products purchased at another *fixed* date. But the meaning of the 'budget equation' is that these two kinds of payments must be simultaneous. In strict logic Walras's model is timeless: *all* transactions take place at a point of time, at the equilibrium system of prices (which was established beforehand); as all prices are 'market clearing', the intermediation of money appears otiose. Walras, who grafts money as *encaisse désirée* to his general equilibrium system at a late stage, makes no real attempt to show how it can be fitted into it.

become a certain multiple of the quantity of commodity-money, and thereby decrease the value of the money-commodity as compared to what it would have been in the absence of those innovations.[7] However, so long as a strict proportionality is maintained between changes in the quantity of 'real money' and the outstanding amount of money substitutes, 'the theorem of the proportionality of prices to the quantity of "real" money is not affected in any way by the existence of paper circulation and payments by offsets (i.e. by the clearing of cheques)'.[8]

10. This last statement of Walras (inserted in his book in the fourth edition in 1900) encapsulates the essence of the modern monetarist position. For it says that so long as money-substitutes of various kinds are in a fixed and constant proportion to real money (i.e. gold or silver), the 'money supply' can be treated as exogenous — i.e. the supply of money is determined independently of the demand for it in the same way as when precious metals were the sole means of payment.[9] And since the Walrasian economy functions with the full and efficient utilization of scarce resources (which of course means far more than 'full employment' as generally understood),[10] (i) a rise in the price-level can only occur in a state of excess demand for commodities *in general*; (ii) such an 'excess demand' only arises, given the stability of the public's demand for cash balances, when the money supply increases faster than the supply of commodities in general, and hence the value of the money-commodity falls in relation to all others.

[7] Walras states this as if it were an obvious implication of the existence of money-substitutes: but he does so in a hesitant manner, emphasising that 'promises to pay' cannot be regarded as fully equivalent to *real* money. Nor does he face up to the consequences that the equilibrium conditions require that the value of money should correspond to the cost of production of the money-commodity in terms of other commodities — which would argue against the view that the invention of money-substitutes changes the value of the money-commodity in terms of other commodities.

[8] See Walras, *Elements*, English edition, Lesson 33, p. 336.

[9] This view overlooks the fact that the *emergence* of money-substitutes — whether in the form of bank notes, bank accounts, or credit cards — was a spontaneous process, not planned or regulated 'from above' by some central authority, and for that reason alone it is impossible to treat some arbitrary definition of money (which includes specific forms of such money-substitutes in the definition of money) as an exogenous variable. The emergence of surrogate money was a spontaneous process resulting from the development of the banking system; this development brought a steady increase in the ratio of money substitutes of 'real' money; it is impossible, therefore, to regard the one as being a constant multiple of the other.

[10] It assumes not just the full employment of labour, but an optimal allocation of labour and other resources which alone makes the production of goods in the aggregate *wholly* supply-constrained.

11. The modern monetarists – at least those of them who have thought about the matter sufficiently to reach a logically consistent position – follow Walras in three essential respects.

(1) They assume that the economy left to itself is 'self-regulating' and functions so as to ensure the full utilization of resources. This implies that the markets in the real world behave like 'Walrasian markets', and that means, in turn, that they operate under conditions of universal perfect competition, complete flexibility of prices both upwards and downwards, and all markets 'clear' – there are no unsatisfied buyers or sellers.

(2) They assume that there is *no* important difference between the functioning of a commodity-money economy and a credit-money economy. In the latter money consists of transferable certificates of debt ('promises to pay') which are convertible only into other kinds of 'promises to pay', and which come into existence as a by-product of open market operations of the Central Bank and of credit created by the banking system, and *not* as a result of income-generating productive activity.

(3) They assume that successful control of the growth of the money supply will *in itself* exert a 'downward pressure' on prices and thereby moderate the rate of inflation and indeed bring it to an end if the control is maintained long enough.

1. REASONING FROM FALSE PREMISSES

12. The first assumption leads to a failure to recognize the all-important difference between a demand-inflation and a cost-inflation. In the 'Walrasian' model of the economy, a rise in prices *can* occur *only* as a result of excess demand in some or all the markets. Costs (or incomes generated in the process of production) in that model of the economy are *derived* from prices; they cannot therefore exert an autonomous influence on prices. In the real world, however, except in circumstances where there is an excessive pressure on resources due to excessive demand (this generally happens as a result of a major war or its aftermath) prices of goods and of services (at least in the industrial sector) rise in consequence of a rise in costs – such as the cost of raw materials, fuel, or labour – and each cost-induced rise in prices tends to generate further price and cost increases, even in circumstances in which there is an excess supply of labour and of productive capacity.

13. The second assumption carries the implication that money has

an 'exogenous' supply schedule which determines the quantity available independently of the demand for it (in the same way as with commodity-money, whether it consists of units of gold, silver, or oxen), and for that reason its relative scarcity directly determines its value in relation to other commodities — since it is only through the reduction in the value of money that the additional 'supply' can find 'takers' — i.e. that the rise in its quantity can be matched by a corresponding increase in the public's desire to hold money. In fact, under a 'credit-money' system such un-wanted or excess amounts of money *could never come into existence*; it is the increase in the value of transactions — whether it is due to a rise in costs or in the volume of production or both — which calls forth an increase in the 'money supply' (whether in the form of bank balances or notes in circulation) as a result of the net increase in the value of work-ing capital at the various stages of production and distribution.

14. The third assumption implies that the quantity of money and the velocity of circulation are mutually invariant to each other — whereas in reality monetary controls which succeed in reducing the money stock (or cause it to rise at a lower rate) may only succeed in causing the public to economize on cash holdings (i.e. to reduce Walras's 'desired cash balances' at a given level of incomes) without affecting the level of expenditures. The monetarists, in strict analogy to Walras, assume that the superstructure of credit money varies in strict propor-tion to 'basic money' whether the latter is thought of as gold in the vaults of the Central Bank or simply as the amount of bank notes printed by the Central Bank and brought into circulation through the discounting of 'eligible' bills and/or through open market operations.[11] If this were the case, the Central Bank would clearly determine, month by month, or week by week, how much money *should* exist (whether defined as M1, M3, or M7) simply by regulating the issue of banknotes. In that situation there would be no problem of ensuring the fulfilment of monetary 'targets': they would be *automatically* fulfilled by fixing or 'rationing' the volume of banknotes issued every day.[12] However, in

[11] The notion of banknotes issued or 'in circulation' includes of course balances of the clearing banks with the Central Bank which are fully equivalent to it.

[12] The Bank Act of 1844 imposed the condition that the issue of bank notes in excess of a fixed amount (called the fiduciary issue) must be fully backed by gold — an increase in the note issue could only occur therefore as a result of an inflow of gold from abroad. In the latter part of the 19th century the Bank was able to exercise a discretionary policy by inducing a movement of funds between financial centres through variations in its rate of discount (in the Bank Rate) relatively to other financial centres.

fact, the Bank cannot *refuse* the discounting of 'eligible bills' rendered
to it by the discount houses. If it did, by setting a fixed limit to the
amount which the Bank is prepared to discount on a daily or a weekly
basis (in the same way as the box office of a theatre is willing to sell
a fixed number of tickets for a performance) the Bank would fail in
its function as 'lender of last resort' to the banking system which is
essential to ensure that the clearing banks do not become insolvent as
a result of a lack of liquidity. Precisely because the monetary authorities
cannot afford the disastrous consequences of a collapse of the banking
system, while the banks in turn cannot allow themselves to get into
a position of being 'fully stretched', the 'money supply' in a credit-
money economy is *en*dogenous, not *ex*ogenous − it varies in direct
response to changes in the public 'demand' to hold cash and bank
deposits and not independently of that demand.[13]

15. This is implicitly recognized in ministerial pronouncements and
in official documents − as, for example, the recent joint memorandum
by the Treasury and the Bank of England on Monetary Control[14] −
which emphasized that the control over the money supply operates
indirectly by influencing the public's demand for money and not by
directly controlling the supply. It is evident in the Chancellor's statement that 'monetary policy is essentially a medium term policy', and

[13] For a convincing demonstration of why the 'money supply' is endogenous
in a credit money economy (in contrast to a commodity-money economy) see
J. R. Hicks, 'Monetary Experience and the Theory of Money', in *Economic
Perspectives* (Oxford, 1977). Milton Friedman (and other monetarists) fully
recognize that the monetarist view of inflation entirely depends on the assumption that the money supply is *ex*ogenous (i.e. that changes in the money stock are
a cause, and not a consequence, of the change in incomes and prices). He admits
(at least he did in his 1970 note in the *Lloyd's Bank Review* − whether he still
does is perhaps open to question) that 'in a scientific problem the final verdict is
never in − any conclusion must always be subject to revision in the light of new
evidence'. However, at different points in time he relied on different *kinds* of
evidence to support the same hypothesis: his basic view has never changed, although
the evidence adduced in support of it underwent numerous transformations. Thus
for many years he relied on the supposed existence of a time-lag − i.e. that
changes in the money stock *invariably* precede changes in money incomes (which
incidentally is very dubious) − for proving the direction of causality. But later,
under the influence of critics, he retreated from that position, asserted that he
never intended it to be proof of causality, and was ready to 'expunge it altogether',
from the list of reasons for the supposed exogeneity of the money supply. (See
his reply to Tobin, *Quarterly Journal of Economics*, May 1970, pp. 321-2.) As
for the nature of the evidence supplied in his latest book (Milton and Rosa
Friedman, *Free to Choose − A Personal Statement* (London, 1980), see the letter
to *The Times* by Professors Hahn and Neild, 13 March 1980 (Business Page).
[14] The Green Paper on *Monetary Control* (HMSO, March 1980), Cmnd. 7858.

that its 'main instruments *must continue to be* fiscal policy and interest rates'[15] (whilst no mention is made of fixing a limit to the volume of banknotes put into circulation).

16. These instruments operate, not on the supply, but on the public's *demand* for money and on their desire to hold assets in monetary form – either directly, by changing the public's desire to hold bank deposits in preference to other financial assets, or indirectly, by influencing the level of expenditures on consumption and investment and, through the latter, the change in money incomes and *hence* the transaction demand for holding cash and bank deposits.

17. These two mechanisms – the direct and the indirect – are best considered separately. It is the first mechanism – i.e. the measures taken to discourage the holding of assets in monetary form – which lends the policy a distinct 'monetarist' flavour, but, as I hope to show, it is only the second mechanism which holds out any prospect of influencing the rate of inflation.

2. THE ROLE OF THE PSBR

18. In the Green Paper on Monetary Control of March 1980 it is asserted that 'it is sometimes helpful to examine how a particular control will affect items on the asset side of the banking system'. The Paper then proceeds to state an accounting identity which shows the change in the money stock (£M3) in a given period as the sum of five separately identified items, of which the PSBR is one (though it is not claimed that the five items are mutually invariant).

19. In my view it may be more helpful to view the effects of the PSBR on the asset side of the non-banking private sector, both at home and overseas. The PSBR in any year can be defined as the public sector's net de-cumulation of financial assets (net dissaving) which by accounting identity must be equal to the net acquisition of financial assets (net saving) of the private sector, home and overseas; which in turn can be broken down to the net acquisition of financial assets of the personal sector, of the company sector, and the overseas sector (the latter is the negative of the balance of payments on current account). Ignoring capital flows of *existing* wealth to and from the country, the change in the liabilities of the banking system is thus equal to that part of the net saving (or the net increment of financial assets) of the

[15] See the Chancellor's letter to the Committee of 18 February 1980; Cmnd. 7858, Introduction, para. 4. (Italics not in the original.)

home and overseas private sector which persons and companies wish to hold in the form of sterling bank deposits as against other financial assets (such as 'bonds' or 'gilts') and which in turn is equal to that part of the PSBR which is financed by the addition of the banking system's holding of public sector debt.

20. The main monetarist thesis is that the net dissaving of the public sector is 'inflationary' in so far as it is 'financed' by the banking system and *not* by the sale of debt (bonds or gilts) to the public. But this view ignores the fact that the net saving, or net acquisition of financial assets of the *private* sector will be the same irrespective of whether it is held in the form of bank deposits or of bonds. The part of the current borrowing of the public sector which is directly financed by net purchases of public debt by the banking system — and which has its counterpart in a corresponding increase in bank deposits held by the non-banking private sector — is just as much part of the net saving of the private sector as the part which is financed by the sale of gilts to the private sector. When the public sector's de-cumulation of financial assets increases (i.e. the PSBR increases) there must be an equivalent increase in the net savings of the non-bank private sector (home and overseas) as compared with what net savings would have been with an unchanged PSBR[16] which will be the same irrespective of how much of that saving takes the form of purchases of gilts and how much takes the form of an increase in deposits with the banking system. The decision of how much of the increment in private wealth is held in one form or another is a portfolio decision depending on relative yields, the expectation of future changes in interest rates (long and short), and the premium which the owners are willing to pay for 'liquidity' — i.e. the possession of command over resources in a form that can be directly applied to extinguish debts or to meet financial commitments.

21. But it is a mistake to think that an individual's spending plans (whether in a business or in a personal capacity) are significantly affected by the decision of how much of his wealth he decides to keep in the

[16] It is sometimes suggested that the 'inflationary' effect of financing the PSBR through the issue of 'bills' rather than the sale of gilts resides in the fact that bills constitute a 'reserve asset' of the banks who are thereby enabled to extend more credit to the private sector than they would otherwise. This would be true only if the so-called Reserve Assets Ratio (of $12\frac{1}{2}$ per cent) had been 'designed to serve as an officially-controlled monetary base' which we are assured has not been the case (see Cmnd. 7858, para. 3.6., also Annex A). It is possible that the rise in the PSBR merely serves to offset (fully or in part) the fall in net savings that would otherwise have occurred as a result of a fall in private home investment or in net foreign investment (i.e. in the current account balance).

form of 'money' (broadly or narrowly defined) as against other financial assets that are easily convertible into money (including available overdraft facilities). It is equally mistaken (in my view) to assume that the part of current private saving which is held in the form of additional bank deposits gives rise to additional lending by the banks to the private sector, whereas the part which is held in the form of bonds does not. In the former case the increase in the banks' liabilities to depositors is matched by a corresponding increase in the banks' holding of public sector debt.[17]

22. It is a basic tenet of Keynes's theory that there is an inverse relation between the amount of money individuals desire to hold (as a proportion of income or wealth) and the rate of interest, since the higher the rate the greater the financial sacrifice involved in holding money. These propositions only apply, however, to non-interest-bearing deposits (such as £M1) and not to interest-bearing deposits on which moreover (in the case of Britain) the payment of interest moves in close relation to MLR and money-market rates. A rise in interest rates which makes the holding of M1 less attractive makes the holding of interest-bearing deposits (M3—M1) more attractive relative to gilts, since their yield increases more than that of gilts.[18]

23. It is by no means evident, therefore, that a rise in short-term interest rates will reduce the demand for money on the *broad* definition of money which everyone agrees is the only suitable 'target' for monetary policy. But even if it did — as would happen, for example, if the Bank and the Treasury adopted 'Regulation Q' of the Federal Reserve and put a ceiling on interest rates payable to depositors, irrespective of the market rates — it would mean no more than that the public would be induced to economize in the use of money. It would imply a corresponding rise in the velocity of circulation of money but would not cause any change in spending decisions.[19]

---

[17] The purpose of the introduction of 'Competition and Credit Control' was to allow the banks to lend as much as there is demand for at the prevailing interest rates; given the amounts for which borrowers can be found, the techniques of 'liability management' ensure that the reserve ratio requirements are also fulfilled. (In fact these requirements are due to be abolished in any case: Cmnd. 7858, para. 3.8)

[18] See Table III for empirical evidence that in both Britain and the US the demand for money is positively related (not, as Keynes supposed, negatively) to the rate of interest (on the broad definition which includes interest-bearing deposits as part of the money supply). On the confusion caused by Keynes's terms 'money' and the 'rate of interest' in the *General Theory* see also para. 71.

[19] There are numerous ways of economizing in the holding of 'cash' e.g. through

24. If this were really so, it would be pointless (or ineffective) to use the instrument of interest rate variation as a regulator of the 'money supply'. But there is another aspect to the matter. A change in interest rates will affect the relative attractiveness of holding money (or bills) on the one hand and bonds (or gilts) on the other hand, since these depend not only on the current redemption yields but on the expected variation of interest rates, both short and long, in the future. If the authorities raise MLR soon enough and *far enough* to create the expectation that the prevailing short rates (and *hence* the prevailing gilt-edged yields) are *temporarily* high − i.e. that they are higher than the average to be expected in the longer term − then the holding of long-dated gilts becomes relatively more attractive.[20] In these circumstances the authorities are able to induce the public to switch into new issues, and there can be little doubt that the opportunities for 'funding' afforded by increases in interest rates *which are regarded as temporary* are a far more powerful instrument for keeping the growth of the 'money supply' within the target range than the effect of interest rate changes as such.

25. However, the effect of introducing publicly-announced official 'targets' for the money supply makes the conduct of monetary policy *more* difficult in so far as this enables the market to anticipate future movement of interest rates before the authorities think it appropriate to act. As the Green Paper says, 'If the money supply starts to grow faster than the target range, investors will expect interest rates to rise and so hold back from buying gilts; this further accelerates the growth of the money supply.'[21] Indeed, by delaying their normal purchases of gilts in line with the current accrual of funds, the investment managers of insurance companies and pension funds are able to hold the authorities to ransom. By keeping current accruals (which are very

a synchronization of the timing of payments, increased use of credit cards, giro, etc. These may change the distribution of credits (or debts) as between particular individuals and businesses on any particular 'day', but not their total amount.

In practice, the demand for bank balances of both kinds − that is to say, £M3 − as distinct from non-interest-bearing demand deposits (£M1) appears if anything to show a perverse relationship to changes in interest rates, in that the rise in interest-bearing deposits, following upon higher interest rates, tends, on the whole, to more than offset the fall in non-interest-bearing deposits. For evidence for the UK and US see Table III.

[20] In the words of the Green Paper, 'greater importance is attached (by the market) to the prospect of capital gains or losses than to the immediate interest cost of short-term funds' (Annex A, para. 4).

[21] Ibid., para. 1.4.

large — something of the order of £800 millions per month) temporarily in the form of deposits, they cause the money supply to rise faster than it would otherwise, and thereby force the authorities to raise the MLR and subsequently make new issues on more favourable terms.

26. On the other hand, if the authorities raise interest rates *before* the market expects that to happen (as was the case last November) they are likely to succeed in giving the impression that interest rates are at a temporary 'crisis level' which may cause investment managers to become anxious not to miss the bus, and to take up new issues with unseemly haste — as was shown by the remonstrations of frustrated lenders in the Bank's corridors on some recent occasions.

27. Quite irrespective of that, the market may regard any MLR rate which is higher than, say, 12 per cent, as strictly temporary — for no more sophisticated reason than that in the past such rates were never maintained for more than a few months.[22] Under the 'old' rules of the game, Bank Rate was raised and lowered according to the in- or outflow of Bank reserves, or sometimes according to movement in the balance of payments on current account (these two criteria were themselves highly correlated). The experience with the new criterion of varying MLR with the movement of £M3 relative to target has been too short to give rise to different expectations. Hence a 'negative yield gap' (i.e. when long-dated gilts have a *lower* yield than bank deposits or money market rates) only occurred in the past for short periods. Since early 1979, however, and particularly since the advent of the new Government, there opened up a 'negative yield gap' between bonds and bills which, as far as I can tell, is quite unprecedented in spread, intensity, and duration. Since last November the yields of 'irredeemable' stock, $2\frac{1}{2}$ per cent Consols, fell to 5 per cent *below* MLR; the yield of stock of 7-20 years maturity to $3-3\frac{1}{2}$ per cent below; that of five years' maturity or less to $2-2\frac{1}{2}$ per cent below. All this is only explicable on the supposition that the market has been continually expecting a fall in MLR; with the passage of time these expectations have become stronger and more persistent. They occurred moreover in spite of a veritable flood of new issues of gilts; cash issues net of redemptions to the non-bank private sector amounted to £9.4 billions in the financial year in 1979–80 (including £1.1 billion to the overseas sector), which was only very little less than the PSBR of £9.8 billions of that year.

[22] Rates above 12 per cent were in operation for four months in 1973–4, for six months in 1976–7, for four months in 1978–9 and now for twelve months since June 1979 (last rise to 17 per cent in November 1979).

Indeed, for the last three financial years prior to 1979–80 the amount 'funded' through net new issues to the non-banking private sector was £24.3 billions, while the cumulative PSBR for these years was only £24.7 billions, or £0.3 billion more.[23] This makes complete nonsense of the frequent assertions of Treasury Ministers that the PSBR is a 'major' cause of the increase in the money supply or that 'funding' (i.e. borrowing from the non-bank private sector) requires 'ever increasing rates of interest' or that 'inflationary expectations' are a major factor determining interest rates. The fact is that the PSBR, when allowance is made for borrowing from outside the banking system, was responsible for only 2 per cent of the growth of the money stock for the last three years and only 8 per cent of the growth of the money stock for the last four years. The fact that this borrowing occurred despite an increasingly negative yield gap shows that so far from the public requiring to be tempted by 'ever increasing rates of interest', they are ready to plunge in despite the much higher immediate return obtainable on bank deposits and other liquid assets. The fact that they were ready to lend well below the money market rates, even on 'shorts' of less than five years' maturity, shows *either* that they do not believe that inflation will last more than a very short period, *or* (which is more likely) that the portfolio decisions concerning the distribution of holdings between cash and bonds depends only on expectations concerning future interest rates, and not on expectations concerning future prices.[24]

28. Thus, as a result of the Bank's policies concerning funding, the money supply ceased to bear any relationship whatsoever to changes in PSBR — contrary to frequent ministerial pronouncements that the two are closely related.[25] Nor, on the monetarists' own theory, could the public sector deficit have played any role in inflation. This was achieved, however, at the cost of burdening future governments with large obligations of interest payments[26] — for the new issues, though

[23] See *Financial Statistics*, Tables 2.6, 3.9, and 7.3 Net issues of gilt edged for cash were £11,525 m., of which however £2.634 m. were absorbed by public funds and other public sector transactions whilst UK banks and the discount market *released* (net) £384 m., leaving £8.325 m., to the UK non-bank private sector and £1,099 m. to the overseas sector.

[24] This issue is further discussed in paras. 102–3.

[25] As the regression equation in Table X shows, there was no correlation whatever between the PSBR or the 'unfunded' PSBR and the growth of £M3 in the period 1966–79. For the period 1954–68, on the other hand (which preceded monetarist policies), the correlation coefficient was $R^2:0.740$, with a regression coefficient equal to unity. (See *Lloyd's Bank Review*, July 1970, p. 18.)

[26] These burdens are 'large' on the assumption that 'Governments' (either this

they had much lower coupons than the current MLR, are still pretty high (around 11-12 per cent) by historical standards — and of allowing large short-term gains to successful operators who could re-sell partly-paid stock which they succeeded in subscribing to, sometimes with a 30 to 50 per cent gain in twenty-four hours.

29. In fact high interest cost is by no means an inevitable consequence of a policy of large-scale funding. By setting a low ceiling to interest payable on deposits (or by creating a downward pressure on these rates through a more drastic use of Supplementary Special Deposits) funding could be made attractive to the market at much lower yields — as is shown by the experience of the last war, when despite an enormously larger PSBR (as a percentage of GNP) the Government succeeded in funding much the greater part of its borrowing requirement with long and medium dated issues which had a redemption yield of around $3-3\frac{1}{2}$ per cent.

30. There is no doubt that 'funding' is an efficient instrument for reducing the growth of the money stock, and one which could be pursued indefinitely — or as long as any short-term debt is left out-standing. The question is, so what? Why *should* a given budgetary deficit be less inflationary in its consequences if the debt is funded that if it is not funded — remembering that the additional savings created by the income-generating effect of the public sector deficit are the same in both cases? This question goes to the heart of the monetarist versus non-monetarist controversy. The true monetarist believes that through an unknown and undisclosed mechanism — through the operation of a 'black-box' — the progressive reduction of the rate of growth of the money supply, whether broadly or narrowly defined, exerts a 'down-ward pressure on prices' which, if sustained long enough, must inevitably bring inflation to an end[27] (though with a variable time-lag which is put at between six months and two years). Until it is shown how this mechanism operates it is no better than a fairy-tale, or a mystique which, among primitive peoples, takes the form of endowing particular objects, like a tree, or a mountain, with magic powers.

one or the next one) will succeed in bringing inflation to a halt. Assuming the continuance of inflation at something like the present rates, the terms of borrowing have of course been very favourable to the community at large.

[27] See for example, Cmnd. 7858, Introduction.

IV. HOW THE POLICY REALLY FUNCTIONS

31. To make sense of the Government's strategy we must now describe the second of the two mechanisms mentioned in para. 17 above. This second mechanism is identical in its mode of operation with Keynesian methods of demand management: the difference is not in the use of instruments but in the objectives of policy. Keynesian demand management aims at securing a constant pressure of demand which is judged sufficient to secure the full utilization of resources but not large enough to generate inflation through excess demand. The present Government uses these instruments, not in order to secure full employment but to create enough unemployment to bring the trade unions to heel, and thereby bring the level of pay settlements sufficiently below the current rate of price inflation to bring about a steady and gradual abatement in the rate of cost inflation. A strongly over-valued pound, by narrowing the market for British-made goods both at home and abroad, is a critical element in this process, which is probably far more important quantitatively than the direct discouragement of high interest rates to short- or long-term investment. Fiscal policy (expressed in terms of PSBR targets) serves the same end. Both through expenditure cuts and through higher taxes and charges it reduces the real value of the wage packet and thereby curtails consumption demand; it also reduces the net demand effect of public expenditure.

32. By these means the Government has been able to ensure that the market demand for labour is reduced and goes on falling. But for the policy to succeed it is necessary that workers should accept falling real wages — without attempting to restore their real income through compensating increases in money wages. In other words, 'real wage resistance'[28] must be broken. While the initial policy pronouncements of the present Government avoided mentioning wages as a cause of inflation (they simply said that it is up to the workers to choose whether they wish to 'price themselves out of the market' or be content with lower wages) more recent pronouncements laid increasing emphasis on 'moderate pay settlements' — pay settlements which are *below* the going rate of price-inflation — as an essential element in bringing down the rate of increase

[28] See J. R. Hicks, 'What is Wrong with Monetarism', *Lloyd's Bank Review*, October 1975, p. 5.

in prices.[29] The behaviour of wages is frequently attributed to the prevalence of 'inflationary' price expectations. There is no evidence, however (nor any logical reason for supposing), that the wage demands put forward in the collective bargaining process depends on expectations concerning the *future* course of prices, rather than on price increases that have already occurred since the date of the previous settlement. It is past inflation, not the expectation of future inflation, which keeps the wage/price spiral going, driven by its own momentum.[30]

33. Since coming into office, the Government adopted a whole host of measures which had the effect of raising the retail price index. The rise in VAT rates, and other indirect taxes, of interest rates and the cost of mortgages, of high charges for public utilities and social services of various kinds (for prescriptions, school meals, etc.), must have jointly contributed a 6–8 per cent addition to the cost of living. This makes the problem of the 'de-escalation of pay settlements' (which the Chancellor considers essential) far more difficult, since the rise in prices attributable to such factors means that an *escalation* of settlements is required merely to maintain existing living standards.

34. At the same time a whole set of measures have been introduced to weaken the workers' bargaining power. The avowed purpose of the Employment Bill is 'to bring about a change in the balance of bargaining power in industry great enough to give some hope of a reduction in the size of wage settlements'.[31] The Chancellor's letter to the

[29] This is a clear departure from the pure monetarist view according to which the general level of *prices* is determined by the money supply alone, independently of wages or other cost elements; and all that excessive wage increases can do is to cause labour 'to price itself out of the market' – not to cause *prices* to rise, but to reduce the demand for labour, and thus employment, at the given level of prices. Recent Ministerial pronouncements, however, acknowledge that factors like the rise in oil prices, high interest rates, and higher indirect taxes, as well as high labour costs, will be passed on in the form of higher prices. This is an implicit admission of the existence of 'cost-induced' inflation which proceeds independently of the behaviour of monetary aggregates. (According to the true monetarist doctrine, if the money supply is given, the rise of some prices, like the price of oil, necessarily carries with it the fall of other prices.)

[30] The main reason for this is that owing to time lags and to differences in the frequencies of adjustment of prices to changes in costs, at any one *point* of time there are a number of price increases in the pipeline which reflect cost-increases (due to higher wage rates or fuel and raw material costs) that have already occurred but which are not yet reflected (or not fully) in the prices of finished goods; there are also some wages which fall temporarily behind the wages of other (comparable) workers because their current wage is the result of a settlement arrived at some time ago. See also para. 46.

[31] *Daily Telegraph*, leading article, 2 June 1980.

Committee carries the same implication in saying that the reforms to be effected in the Employment Bill have been designed to 'restore a broad balance of power in the framework for collective bargaining'.

35. The deliberate attempt to lower the living standards of workers is bound to strengthen their *resolve* to resist by the threat of strike action, etc. The measures enumerated above, together with the massive increase in unemployment, are bound to curtail the workers' *ability* to resist. As there is no real precendent in Britain for a Government embarking on a policy of deflation with the explicit object of bringing down the rate of pay settlements to a non-inflationary level, it is impossible to predict the outcome.

36. If the Government succeeds in its object, it is likely to do so by causing wages to fall behind in 'weak sectors' such as the motor industry, as against the 'strong sectors' such as the miners, electricity workers, etc. Past experience suggests that the 'tattered' wage-structure that would emerge from this process is not likely to be viable, and the workers in the disadvantaged sectors will take every opportunity to regain their normal status in the scale of relative earnings. But this implies in turn that any alleviation of inflation brought about in this manner is not likely to be lasting.

37. The Government can point to some success in this policy in the relatively low pay settlements arrived at in the Talbot factories and at British Leyland. In these cases the workers have clearly realized that if they insisted on maintaining their real wage, the losses of the firm would have meant the complete closure of the plants. They also realize that the Government is falling behind its time-table; to generate enough unemployment to cause a collapse of real wage resistance, the rise in unemployment must become much faster than hitherto.

38. With the further weakening of manufacturing industry, the closure of factories and the creation of redundancies are bound to be speeded up — particularly in the 40 per cent of industry represented by the steel, engineering, transport, and shipbuilding complex. But the inherent weakness of the strategy resides in the fact that in order to bring about a marked reduction in the size of pay settlements the employer must be brought to bankruptcy, or at least to the verge of bankruptcy. It is not, therefore, a viable method of restoring a 'broad balance of power in a framework of collective bargaining'. It is a method of ruining *both* sides of industry at the same time, and not of strengthening one side at the expense of the other.

39. In all this, the 'money supply', which is supposed to play such

a key role in the sequence of events, is really no more than a fig-leaf (or at best a smoke-screen). As we have indicated, it is the view of the present Government that the money supply exerts a 'downward pressure' on prices[32] and thus tends to counteract the 'upward pressure' resulting from the action of the Middle East oil producers, the British trade unions, and HMG's 'hard' policies concerning taxes and charges. In fact the 'downward pressure' on prices exerted by the money supply is non-existent – it is a figment of the imagination. A downward pressure on prices, in so far as it exists, comes from the loss of price leadership of British firms to foreign producers in the home market, and not just in foreign markets,[33] which results from the over-valuation of the pound, the absence of trade barriers, and the rapid fall of the home producers' market share in the home market. It is aggravated by the steady weakening of the financial position of firms, brought about by a progressive reduction in the effective demand for products of all kinds attained through a combination of deflationary fiscal measures, and the special 'squeeze' on British firms secured by the over-valuation of the pound (which in turn is maintained by high interest rates). It is a policy of cutting off your nose to spite your face – of progressively ruining private enterprise for the sake of weakening the bargaining power of labour.*

40. The reason for this, as any industrialist would confirm, is that in the short period (and *a fortiori* in the long period) average unit labour costs fall with increasing production until full capacity utilization is reached. For any position short of that point the 'marginal product' of labour exceeds the average product, so that when all workers are paid the same wages, the *highest* profit is earned on the marginal worker (or the marginal unit of output) and not the lowest profit as neo-classical theory would have it.[34] It therefore always *pays* the manufacturer to produce as much as he can sell, even when the price is 'dictated' to him by the market. In circumstances in which the manufacturer is a 'price-follower' and must hold his selling price at or below those of his rivals, a rise in costs, whether due to a rise in

[32] See Cmnd. 7858, Introduction, para. 3.

[33] The usual case is that in the larger industrial countries the main domestic producer is the price leader and the importers (as well as smaller domestic firms) are price followers.

[34] This remains true even though the firm may have a great deal of over-manning, and hence a low productivity curve. But over-manning does not change the *slope* of the curve (only the height) and it is something that reduces profits, irrespective of the ratio of wages to prices.

wages or a rise in interest rates on working capital, while reducing his profits as a share of value added, will not cause him to dismiss a worker so long as any profit is left, since his profit would be further reduced by doing so.[35] Hence high interest rates only bring about a rise in unemployment directly through factory closures.† The bankruptcy of employers is the price the Government must pay in order to reduce the level of demand and to weaken union power through higher unemployment.

41. I am not suggesting that the ministers responsible for this policy are conscious of its effects or consequences. They may truly believe that rigid adherence to the 'monetary targets', if maintained long enough, will ultimately strengthen the economy by 'squeezing inflation out of the system'. But if so, recent pronouncements concerning the need for 'moderation of pay settlements' as a means of hastening the process show a strange lack of consistency – it is an echo from the old days when the 'money supply' was *not* regarded as the instrumental variable capable of producing the desired result on its own.

42. As a result of the mistaken theories and policies of the present Government, the rate of inflation in Britain accelerated by more than could be explained by the breakdown of incomes policy in the winter of 1979. The pay round of 1978-9 (ending in July–August 1979) showed a twelve-monthly rate of wage inflation of 16.5 per cent, which was only 2 per cent above the previous pay round (ending July–August 1978). But the September pay round of 1979-80 showed an annual rate of increase of 22 per cent during July–August, which meant a rise of 6 per cent (as against the 2 per cent increase in the previous pay round mentioned above), some of which resulted from the very large increase of civil servants' pay under the Clegg awards. [From then on the Government operated an unofficial but very firm 'incomes policy' for all public employees, and urged the private employers' organizations to do the same. Assisted by the widespread threat of factory closures and the increase in unemployment to nearly 3 million,

---

[35] It is a different matter when the manufacturer is forced to reduce output on account of a fall in his order books or in sales. Then it pays him to dismiss all those workers not needed for a smaller output – though the number of workers who become redundant in this way must always be a lower proportion of total employees than the proportionate fall in production. However, a rise in labour costs due to a rise in wages or in interest costs on working capital will *not* cause redundancies until the rise in costs reaches the point at which profits become negative, in which case the manufacturer will be better off by closing the plant altogether.

the annual rise in earnings in the last quarter of 1980 and in 1981 fell steadily, month by month, reaching a minimum of 12.1 per cent in July.[36]]

V. THE PROBLEM OF ALTERNATIVE STRATEGIES

43. For reasons already indicated — the varying frequency of price adjustments to the rise in costs, and the spread of the annual wage adjustments around the year from September to July — it is difficult to bring a wage-induced inflation to a halt, once the wage/price spiral attains the dimension of 20 per cent a year or more. In Britain statutory and voluntary incomes policies succeeded in diminishing inflation for periods of several years (since the attempt in 1948), the most successful of them being the policy initiated by Mr Healey and Mr Jack Jones in July 1975, which brought the annual inflation rate from 25 per cent to 7.3 per cent in three years; in the fourth year, however, it broke down.[37] In 1980 it was resuscitated in a concealed form under very different circumstances, and it remains to be seen whether the current trend to lower wage settlements would be maintained for any length if the state of the economy showed any substantial improvement.

44. However, each of these incomes policies was invariably introduced as a temporary emergency measure, with the implicit promise that free collective bargaining would be restored once inflation rates had come down; the ending of such periods on the other hand generally resulted in an acceleration of wage increases *above* price increases. Moreover, on the type of incomes policy pursued by the last and the present Government any substantive reduction of inflation is a 'medium term target'.

45. As against that it has been argued (by Professor Hayek in *The Times* of 5 March 1980, supported by me in the *Guardian* of 11 March 1980) that in the past *great inflations* were almost invariably brought to an end suddenly, and not gradually; this was true of the great German inflation in 1923, the Austrian and Hungarian inflation in

[36] [The passage in square brackets was inserted for the present edition.]

[37] The mere continuation of the Government's economic policies would have made further economic stagnation inevitable and the normal productivity increases might not have occurred. In addition the world prices of primary products and fuel appeared to have shown an increase of the same order — around 15 per cent per year — which now appear to rise at an even faster rate as a result of the large price increases by OPEC producers in 1979.

1924, and the post-World-War II inflation of Hungary, Greece, and Japan, and numerous examples could be found in the history of Latin American inflations, though in some of them the inflation flared up again some years later.

46. However, the common characteristic of all these cases has been that the rate of increase in prices reached the dimensions of a 'hyper-inflation' (of several hundred per cent a year) before it suddenly came to a halt. Like the great plagues of the past, they burnt themselves out. The question is why? I think the explanation — it is a hypothesis which would require a great deal of research to test — is that the faster the inflation, the more prices and incomes become 'indexed' to inflation; and while the spread of indexing tends to accelerate inflation considerably, it also shortens the lag of adjustments of prices to costs, and of wages and salaries to prices; the smaller that lag, the weaker are the forces that keep the wage/price spiral going. Thus in Germany in September 1923, everything from newspapers to railway tickets and to daily wages was 'indexed' to the daily market price of the US dollar (there was no time to calculate the daily change in the retail price index!) so there was no accumulated backlog of wage and price adjust-ments left. If the dollar price remained unchanged for a day, prices and wages (expressed in billions or trillions of paper marks) remained stable for the day. If the dollar remained stable for a fortnight, the expectation began to spread that inflation was likely to be over, and as the old paper marks were gradually converted to a new 'renten-mark' (secured by a first mortgage of 7 per cent of all immobile private property in Germany — hardly the equivalent of a liquid asset that could be used to stabilize the new currency in the foreign exchange market) the inflation was over for good, or at least until Germany's defeat in 1945.

47. Nobody, I think would advocate hyper-inflation as a cure for inflation — it is like advocating the spread of a highly contagious disease in order to acquire immunity from it.

48. If this avenue is excluded, what is left? The adoption of a *permanent* incomes policy may be the best longer-term solution, but it requires complex new institutional arrangements to replace the pre-vailing systems of wage bargaining; it requires far-reaching consensus and co-operation by the three 'social partners', Capital, Labour, and Government, which is not within the 'art of the possible' in Britain in the short or even the medium term.

49. My alternative strategy would be a package involving radical

measures on five different fronts, *all* of which are required for the success of the scheme:

(1) A statutory freeze of *all* wages, salaries, dividends and rents and *all* prices of home-made goods, for an indefinite period. To prevent forestalling, the Government must bring in a temporary freeze effective immediately on announcement, for, say, thirty days (subject to subsequent affirmative resolution in both Houses of Parliament); this is to be followed by a freeze established by legislation (assuming that it can be passed in time).

(2) A statutory *guarantee* for a minimum reduction in the retail price index of 2 per cent per annum, possible raised to 3 per cent per annum later. In order to fulfil this guarantee the Government should have the powers to adopt any of the following measures or any combination of them:

  (i) An export levy on British oil, coal, or gas, and an import subsidy on the imports of such fuels, necessary to stabilize domestic sterling prices to both industrial and domestic users;

  (ii) A variable import subsidy designed to stabilize the domestic price of imported food and raw materials;

  (iii) Powers given to the Government for a temporary reduction or suspension of indirect taxes, charges, etc. which enter into the cost of living index by Government Order, to the extent necessary to validate the required guaranteed annual reduction in the cost of living.

(3) *Either*

  (a) the introduction of general import controls on all *competitive* imports (imports competing with domestic output) – most manufactures and semi-manufactures but also including co – either by a way of *ad valorem* duties of the kind introduced in the 1932 legislation, or by a licensing system which make all such imports subject to license, the amounts being limited to some percentage (say, 80 or 90 per cent) of the amount actually imported in 1979.

  Or

  (b) the introduction of a system of *dual exchange rates* under which there is a special rate applicable to manufactured imports and exports, the rate of which is two-thirds of the *present* exchange value of the £ in terms of the Smithsonian average, but which would be reduced/increased according as the exchange rate of the £ fell/rose in relation to the Smithsonian average. (Example. If the current rate of sterling is equivalent to 75 per cent of the Smithsonian average, or, say, $2.35 to the £, the special rate applicable to exporters and importers of manufactures would be 50 per cent of the Smithsonian, or $1.566 to the £.) Exporters are entitled to convert foreign exchange at the special rate on a certification of the monthly value of their f.o.b. exports; importers will be required to acquire foreign exchange — or pay the difference in sterling — before getting clearance for their imports.

The difference between the two methods is that the second combines a flat *ad valorem* duty on competitive imports with an equivalent subsidy on exports.[38]

(4) The progressive reduction of interest rates in successive steps, which would have an important cost-reducing effect and would also reduce the cost of living index directly through mortgage rates, etc. There is evidence for believing that interest costs are passed on in higher prices in much the same way as wage costs. This would also serve to lower the exchange value of the £, thus paving the way to the gradual reduction of the difference between the general exchange rate and the special rate applicable to manufactures, with a view to their ultimate elimination.

(5) There should be set up an *Anomalies Commission* (with members appointed by the trade unions, the employers and the Government) whose task would be to examine how far the introduction of the freeze on incomes and prices at the given date distorted the relationship of earnings of different grades and occupations as compared with a moving average of the past five years (or ten years). Having identified the anomalies, the Commission should be empowered to recommend their gradual elimination in a succession of steps consistent with the maintenance of the 2 per cent annual improvement in disposable real incomes in the average, and the maintenance of a constant real income (as a minimum) for those who are 'down-graded' as a result of the rectification process.

) The setting up of a *Monitoring Commission*, with a similar

---

[38] Dual exchange rates (or multiple exchange rates) were in general use by countries of the 'gold bloc' from 1933 onwards, who preferred to maintain the formal gold parity of their currencies but wished to ensure that their exports were competitive with Britain and the US who devalued their currencies in terms of gold. Thus at one time under the system evolved by Dr. Schacht there were over twenty special rates for German marks for the export of specific commodities only. (Thus there were 'aspirin marks', 'bicycle marks', 'toy marks', etc.)

constitution, for monitoring the observance of the anti-inflationary programme, reporting to Parliament at, say, six monthly intervals.

50. The key to the success of the whole scheme is the expansion of the GDP due to higher effective demand resulting from the rise in real disposable income, and the diversion of demand from imported to home-produced goods. The scheme is only viable if the potential for expansion is large. Past experience suggests that it is. When general import controls in the form of protective *ad valorem* duties were introduced at the beginning of 1932, manufacturing output expanded by 7.8 per cent a year in the following five years (or 50 per cent altogether), manufacturing productivity rose by 3.9 per cent a year, and manufacturing employment by 4.1 per cent a year; the rise in the GDP over the five years 1932–7 was 4.7 per cent a year.

51. Of course it can be argued that 1932 was more depressed, and had more surplus capacity, than exists in 1980. Unemployment was 3.4 millions or 15.6 per cent of the labour force. But even if related to the previous peak output of 1929, when unemployment was only 1.5 million or 7.3 per cent of the labour force, the five year improvement from 1932 onwards would still come to $33\frac{1}{3}$ per cent of manufacturing output, or 5.7 per cent a year, and that of the GDP to 3.6 per cent a year. This would leave plenty of scope for import substitution as well as a 2 per cent annual increase in consumption per head.

VI. COMMENTS ON PARTICULAR ISSUES

1. THE SUPPLY SIDE OF THE ECONOMY

52. It has been frequently asserted by the Chancellor and other Ministers that the unsatisfactory level of output in the economy, its stagnation and/or downward trend over time is due to 'supply-side difficulties' rather than to lack of effective demand; they can, therefore, only be remedied by a policy of 'strengthening the supply side' which is the real objective of the Government's anti-inflationary policies, and of policies aimed at 'increasing incentives to work'.

53. The question is, in what sense, if any, the British economy is hemmed in by limitations on the supply side, and if it is, whether the Government's policies are well adapted for easing them or removing them.

54. Two aspects of this question must be sharply distinguished:

(i) The first is the *capacity to produce* as determined by (*a*) available manpower, its abilities and skills, the availability of managerial, technical, and scientific talents; (*b*) the availabilities of physical resources; comprising both land and natural resources and man-made resources in the form of buildings, plant and equipment, means of transport, etc.

(ii) The second question is *the nature of the obstacles* that prevent the fullest utilization of these resources, and whether the Government's present policies are likely to remove them or to aggravate them.

55. As to (i), there can be no question that there is a large amount of unutilized and under-utilized capacity in the British economy, in the form of both open and disguised unemployment[39] and a lot of physical resources which are not fully used. (Excess capacity in steel, engineering, chemical plants, etc. may be 40–50 per cent, if the possibility of multiple shifts in specific areas of shortages of capacity is kept in mind.)

56. In estimating how much this amounts to, as a percentage of the existing GNP, allowance must be made for the time required for eliminating temporary shortages (or 'bottlenecks') which would inevitably arise in a process of re-expansion. Most industrial processes depend to a very large extent on the availability of complementary commodity inputs of raw materials, semi-finished goods, and 'components' (the latter are 'finished' goods which are used only in combination with other commodities). Increased demand for components, etc. is satisfied, in the first instance, by drawing on stocks, the replacement of which requires time (as does the faster adjustment of production for a higher rate of off-take). Hence the stimulus of increased demand will only succeed in reactivating idle resources if (*a*) it proceeds at a relatively gentle pace; (*b*) it is sustained over a long period. In the past, the stimulus administered by 'reflationary policies' (as in the Maudling or Barber booms, or the Butler boom of 1954–5) acted too quickly, and after the early run-down of stocks led to a large influx of imports

[39] The latter is potentially as large or larger than the former. Past experience suggests that an increased demand for the products of manufacturing industries calls forth an increased transference of labour from low-earning sectors (formerly agriculture, now mainly services), where it makes only an insignificant contribution to the social product, and also brings into employment persons (mainly married women) who are willing to take up work if employment opportunities are readily available, but are not active work-seekers. Thus during the period of rapid expansion, 1932–7, total employment increased by 2.6 millions, of which only 1.3 millions came from the reduction of registered unemployed. Employment in manufacturing increased by 1.35 millions or 23 per cent, and in all other sectors of the economy by 9.8 per cent.

(much of which was of temporary nature to bridge the gap until adequate home supplies became available). However, the balance of payments consequences of the resulting import boom generally led to a reversal of policies well before its fruits could fully materialize.[40]

57. It is possible, however, that the failure of the stimulus of demand in activating idle resources is the result, not of temporary bottle-necks, but of a lack of competitiveness of British goods in relation to similar goods made in other countries, either because (a) the costs and prices of British goods are relatively too high when measured in a common currency unit; (b) British goods are inferior to foreign goods on account of quality, design, and other 'non-price' elements of competitiveness, such as after-sales service, availability of spares, delivery dates, etc. Recent studies (by NEDO) show that inferiority in such respects could not easily be compensated by price concessions, and could not therefore be effectively remedied by devaluation. The reactivation of idle resources may be possible only if some form of import controls are introduced.

58. It is possible, therefore, to give an interpretation to the term 'supply difficulties' which refers not to lack of capacity to produce goods, but to *lack of saleability of the goods* produced, part of which is due to the overvaluation of the currency (and which could, in principle, be remedied by a lower exchange rate) and part of it to an inferiority in the quality of British products which cannot be attributed to excessive costs and prices.

59. It is most unlikely, however, that a policy of deflation — i.e. the reduction in the general level of demand through fiscal and monetary measures and through the deliberate overvaluation of the exchange rate — could make a positive contribution to the removal of such impediments. The general argument is that a sharp competitive climate which makes profits harder to earn, and jobs more difficult to find, will call forth greater efficiency in the case of both capital and labour. As against that, it can be argued that an unfavourable business climate in itself militates against efficiency, on account of the loss of produc-

---

[40] It is for this reason that a successful policy of sustained expansion requires either that it be export-led (in which case the additional exports 'finance' the consequential import-boom, and the process can go on without interruption) or else that it is associated, as in 1932, with the introduction of protection (whether in the form of import duties or a licensing system) in which the consequential reduction of 'import propensities' (i.e. the *share* of imports in final expenditure) serves to offset the increase in the volume of imports resulting from the increase in expenditure.

tivity due to a high ratio of overheads to prime costs and the lack of new investment which will inevitably carry with it a lack of design-improvement and product-innovation, and will thus increase the 'unsaleability' of British goods even more. Ultimately it is a question of whether the forces of 'cumulative and circular causation' – by which is meant that success breeds success and failure begets failure – are quantitively more important than the 'static' advantages which argue in favour of a more competitive environment in which the process of 'natural selection' operates more freely.

60. The overwhelming evidence of industrial economies is that progress depends far more on 'success' – i.e. on features favourable to growth, such as buoyant and growing demand – than on greater competitive pressures generated by a harsh business climate.

61. The policy of 'strength through misery' has further innate disadvantages:

(i) First, productivity per head is less, since with low capacity of utilization, overhead costs per unit of output are higher (which is the same as saying that the ratio of overhead labour is higher relatively to labour directly engaged in production). This could be remedied in the long run through a rationalization process which concentrates output on the most efficient plant, abandoning others – but such rationalization processes normally require a common ownership, and their scope is therefore much greater in the public sector (such as coal and steel) than in the private sector.

(ii) The share of profit is low mainly because the margin of profit on prime cost is fixed by reference to a 'standard' or normal ultilization of capacity,[41] and partly also because, on account of the pressure of international competition, higher costs may not be passed on (or not fully) in higher prices.

(iii) The low profit share associated with low capacity utilization militates against investment, on account of both lower incentives, and diminished finance available (retained profits necessarily form the major source of industrial financing).

(iv) If a process of mainly wage-induced inflation is going on (as is likely to be the case at present) the share of wages in GDP *net* of stock-appreciation is likely to be higher than it would be (given

---

[41] See R. R. Neild, *Pricing and Employment in the Trade Cycle* (CUP, 1963); K. Coutts, N. Godley, and W. Nordhaus, *Industrial Pricing in the UK* (CUP, 1978).

the same historical profit margins) in the absence of inflation. This can be put simply by saying that while the inflation goes on, prices lag behind wages (which comes to the same as saying that a larger part of the profit is pre-empted for the payment of the increased cost of replacing stocks) so that, given the level of productivity, the inflation cannot be brought to an end without wages lagging behind prices over a sustained period – i.e. if real wages cannot be reduced during the process of decelerating inflation, owing to workers' resistance to any substantial reduction in their living standards, this alone may frustrate the success of any anti-inflationary policy – unless it is combined with a process reactivating idle resources which enables profits (as a share of output) to rise without a cut in real wages. For that reason alone, the re-expansion of the economy – through the reactivation of idle labour and capital – is the most promising way of bringing inflation to a halt, and the only way of doing this without a cut in real wages.

(v) For reasons just explained, the success of such an expansionist policy presupposes some limitation of 'competitive' imports in any of the ways described in para. 49(3) above. Without *some* form of industrial protection it is most unlikely that inflation can be brought to a halt – whether gradually or suddenly. With protection it can be argued that 'consumers' will be worse off owing to the reduced availability of foreign imports; but they will be better off because of higher employment and earnings; and the latter advantage is bound to weigh more heavily, especially if the policy succeeds not only in reactivating idle resources but in sustaining a higher rate of economic growth.

2. THE MONEY SUPPLY, INTEREST RATES, THE PRICE LEVEL, AND THE PSBR

A. Determinants of the money supply

62. The basic contention of monetarists is that there is a *stable function* of money in relation to income (which comes to the same as saying that there is a stable velocity of circulation, invariant to changes in the quantity of money in circulation). This assertion, first put forward by the early followers of the quantity theory of money in the eighteenth and nineteenth centuries, was denied by Keynes and reasserted by Friedman on the basis of statistical evidence which shows a high

correlation between changes in the amount of money in circulation and changes in the money value of the national income. Friedman admitted, however, that there was nothing in his findings which logically excluded an interpretation diametrically opposite to his own: i.e., that the change in the money supply may be the consequence, not the cause, of the change in money incomes (and prices), and that the mere existence of time-lag — that changes in the money supply *precede* changes in money incomes — is not in itself sufficient to settle the question of causality: one cannot rule out the possibility of an event A which occurred subsequent to B being nevertheless the cause of B (the simplest analogy is the rumblings of a volcano which frequently precede an eruption). Apart from that it is notoriously difficult to establish the existence of a lead of one factor over another, when both move in the same direction in time and the whole question of the existence of a 'lag' is by no means established.[42]

63. In the case of commodity-money, the activities of the mining industry increase the world money supply which is thus determined by factors that are largely independent of the public's demand to hold money. It is possible, therefore (as a result of, say, the discovery of new gold-fields), for additional money to appear which will, in its impact effects, cause a fall in its value relative to other commodities until all the new money finds a 'home' — in the increased balances held by some or all money users.

64. If the proportion of income or expenditure which people wish to hold in the form of money balances (the famous k in the Cambridge quantity equation) is rigidly given, and real income (or output) is also given, the only way in which 'new money' can be absorbed is through a fall in its value in terms of other commodities which, by definition, equals the rise in the value of other commodities in terms of money.[43]

[42] See Table VII for a demonstration that the existence of a time lag of two years or less cannot be established on the available evidence.

[43] Another important factor about commodity-money (which is not true about credit-money) is that an increase in its supply invariably implies either an increase in incomes earned in the production of that commodity (as is the case when new gold-mines are discovered) or at least a capital gain to those who obtain gold by robbery of some kind (as was the case with the sixteenth-century Spaniards). Hence the very addition to the supply of commodity-money implies an increase in the demand for other commodities. In the case of credit money, if the money supply is increased on the initiative of the Central Bank, all that happens is that there is a shift in portfolio holdings with the public holding more money and less bills or bonds. But no one is enriched thereby and therefore no inducement is offered for an increase in the demand for commodities. If on the other hand an increase in the money supply is the result

65. However, with credit-money this kind of problem *cannot* arise, since credit-money comes into existence as a result of borrowing (by businesses, individuals, or public agencies) from the banks; if, as a result of such borrowing, more money comes into existence than the public at the given level of incomes (or expenditures) wishes to hold, the excess gets directly or indirectly repaid to the banks and in this way the 'excess money' is extinguished. In technical parlance, the supply of credit-money is infinitely elastic at the given rate of interest, and this alone rules out the possibility that an 'excess' supply of money relative to demand, or *vice versa*, should be the cause of a 'pressure on prices', upwards or downwards. In a credit-money economy, unlike with commodity-money, supply can never be in excess of the amount individuals wish to hold. The Central Bank has no direct control over the amount of money held by the non-banking public in the form of deposits with the clearing banks; its power is in determining the short rates of interest, either directly through announcing a minimum lending rate (or a re-discount rate), or indirectly through influencing money market rates by open market operations. In the absence of quantitative controls over the clearing banks' lending or borrowing activities, it can only influence the rate of change in the volume of bank deposits held by the public through the effect of changes in interest rates; these effects (for reasons discussed below) are highly uncertain. In the case of credit-money therefore, in contrast to commodity-money, it is *never* true to say that the level of expenditure on goods and services rises in *consequence of* an increase in the amount of bank money held by the public. On the contrary, it is a rise in the level of expenditure which calls forth an increase in the amount of bank money. In a credit-money economy the causal chain between money and incomes or money and prices is the reverse to that postulated by the quantity theory of money.

66. This does not mean that a 'monetarist' economic policy such as that of the present Government is futile. But its real effect depends on the shrinkage of effective demand brought about through high interest rates, an overvalued exchange rate, and deflationary fiscal measures (mainly expenditure cuts), and the consequent diminution is the bargaining strength of labour due to unemployment. Control over the 'money supply' which has in any case been ineffective on the Government's own criteria, is no more than a convenient smoke-screen providing an ideological justification for such anti-social measures.

of increased borrowing from the banks, then the former is the consequence, and not the cause, of the latter.

B. *The definition of money*

67. The meaning of money in everyday parlance comprises everything which is widely used as an instrument for paying for goods and services bought, or for hire of labour or other 'factors of production', which is accepted by the courts as a proper medium for discharging a debt, and by the Government for the payment of taxes. On this definition 'checking accounts' (or current accounts) with any of the clearing banks form part of the 'money supply' of the non-banking public as well as the notes and coins in circulation outside the banking system. The common feature of all these forms of money is that they do not yield interest; they are held purely for convenience. This, roughly, is the definition of £M1. There are, in addition, 'hidden' forms of money which are fully equivalent to money though they are not comprised in the statistics. One of these is travellers cheques outstanding which can be converted into cash at any time; another, and quantitively more important, form consists of unutilized overdraft facilities granted by banks to their customers, which enable the holder to draw upon his account for making payments in excess of his actual credit balance. Finally, there are notes and deposits in foreign currencies which are 'potential money' in the sense that they can be converted into legal tender money at the current rate of exchange, but where the holder bears the risk (or benefits from any gain) of future depreciation or appreciation.

68. In addition to this there are interest-bearing deposits with banks and other financial (or deposit-taking) institutions, which cannot be directly transferred from one person to another, and hence are *not* money, but which can be so easily converted into money that they cannot reasonably be excluded in measuring a person's ability to command resources in terms of general purchasing power. In numerous cases transfers from 'deposit accounts' to 'current accounts' can be effected promptly, without delay; and there can be permanent arrangements by which such transfers are effected automatically by the branch manager (at the end of a week or a month) so as to minimize the interest loss involved in holding checking accounts. For that reason it was always customary to treat deposits of both kinds of the *clearing banks* (i.e. the banks who offer facilities for effecting transfers between accounts by means of cheques issued by the account holder) as part of the 'money supply'. This is now regarded as the preferred definition of a 'policy target' — not because interest-bearing deposits are a means

of payment (which they are not) but simply because they can be so easily converted into media of payment that any 'target' which excludes them is pretty meaningless for policy purposes.

69. However, on this reasoning there is no justification for making any sharp distinction between (interest-bearing) deposits with the clearing banks, and deposits with other banks and deposit-taking financial institutions, such as savings banks, building societies, and 'secondary banks'[44] (which often are no more than a wholly owned subsidiary of one of the main clearing banks). In addition various forms of short-term paper — such as Treasury Bills held outside the banking sector, certificates of deposits or bank-accepted commercial bills so held, and finally gilt-edged of short maturity — are all convertible into cash: either immediately (if they are marketable like bonds or bills) or on giving the customary notice of withdrawal (which is not invariably insisted upon). The conclusion must be, therefore, that once interest-bearing financial assets are admitted as part of the 'money supply' (and for reasons explained, it is impossible to exclude them if the notion of 'controlling the money supply' is to have any credibility) there is no clear demarcation line to be drawn between 'monetary' and 'non-monetary' financial assets. Any *broad* definition of the money supply is therefore arbitrary since it is invariably surrounded by a spectrum of 'liquid assets' which are not comprised in it but which are close substitutes to it.

70. This problem of the definition of 'money' and its consequences was curiously neglected in the literature until it was brought into the open in the Radcliffe Report which took the line that 'while we do not regard the supply of money as an unimportant quantity, we view it as part of the wider structure of the liquidity in the economy. It is the *whole liquidity position* which is relevant to spending decisions . . . spending is not limited by the amount of money in existence'.[45] Until then, British, American, and Continental writers had accepted without question that while a proper definition of the 'money supply' must be

---

[44] The growth of such 'secondary banks' has been greatly stimulated as a result of the so-called 'corset', i.e. the obligation, extending to clearing banks only, to make Supplementary Special Deposits with the Bank of England whenever the growth of their interest-bearing eligible liabilities — i.e. liabilities to the non-banking private sector — exceed a certain target. It is a result of the growth of such avoidance practices that the monetary authorities have now abolished the 'corset' altogether — though without apparently putting anything in its place. See Cmnd. 7858, Chapter 2 (HMSO, 1979). See also para. 121 of this book.

[45] *Report of the Committee on the Working of the Monetary System* (1959), paras. 389–91 (italics not in the original).

much broader than bank notes and coins in circulation, and comprised the means of payments held in the form of bank deposits, this did not invalidate the postulate that the 'money supply', whether a broader or a narrower definition were chosen, is directly controlled by the monetary authority (i.e. the Central Bank) through the control of the 'monetary base', in consequence of which the *supply* of money is exogenously given, independently of the demand for it. The basis of the argument in that given by Walras and quoted in para. 9 above. There were endless disputes between monetary 'experts' as to which of the many 'instruments' of control — the obligatory 'cash ratio' or the 'prudential liquidity ratio', or the 'real' prudential cash ratio of around 2 per cent — was the critical constraint on the relationship between the superstructure of bank money and the underlying 'base money',[46] but these did not call into question the assumption that some instrument exists which makes the 'money supply' invariant with respect to changes in the demand for holding bank deposits.

71. Keynes himself never really questioned the assumption that the *supply of money*, however defined, is exogenously determined by the monetary authorities. At least his equations (whether those in *Treatise in Money* published in 1930, or in the *General Theory* of 1936) are not consistent with any other interpretation.[47] They did not

---

[46] Before World War II there was an obligatory minimum rate of 8 per cent of 'vault cash' plus balances with the Bank of England against the *total* of demand and time deposits. However in practice this was a pious fraud which was habitually circumvented by the simple device of the five big clearing banks making up accounts on different days of the week, from Monday to Friday, so that the *same cash* was exhibited five times a week as it was transferred for accounting purposes from one bank to another each day of the week. The true 'reserve base' (if it existed) was never published though it was known that, for purely prudential reasons, the big clearing banks tried to maintain a minimum 'vault cash' (including their balances with the Bank of England) of around 2 per cent of liabilities. After World War II, the 8 per cent minimum cash ratio was formally abandoned in favour of a 28 per cent liquidity ratio; this however comprised many items, the supply of which were not under the control of the Central Bank at all (such as commercial bills or short-dated bonds) and it was soon recognized that this new 'liquidity ratio' was quite as capable of manipulation as the old cash ratio was. However, despite this, the question of whether the 'money supply' is endogenous to the banking system, and *not* exogenous to it, was not really posed (as far as I know) by any reputable economist writing on the subject, apart from Wicksell and his followers.

[47] The equation $M = L_1(Y) + L_2(r)$ which appears in Keynes's *The General Theory of Employment, Interest and Money* (London, 1936, p. 189), but which could more simply be written $M = L(Y,r)$, assumes M as exogenously given. The Radcliffe Committee's view was that the rate of interest, r, is determined by the monetary authorities while the quantity of money is determined by the desire

concern the supply of money, but the demand for it, which, as described in para. 22 above, he had come to regard as a function of the rate of interest — because the loss of interest is the sacrifice involved in holding money. He considered the 'money supply' in the broad sense and was not troubled by the fact that strictly speaking his liquidity-preference theory only applied to non-interest-bearing deposits.[48]

72. There was no real dissension from the view, according to which the real dividing line between Keynesian and non-Keynesian economics turned on an empirical question: it was concerned with the empirical value of the interest elasticity of the demand for money.[49] In fact the real difference goes much deeper — it concerns the question whether the 'supply side of money', as determined by the monetary authorities, is best represented in terms of the *quantity* of money supplied or in terms of the *interest rate* fixed by the Central Bank, which determines the cost of credit, leaving the quantity outstanding to be determined by demand. If the elasticity of the demand for money in terms of the rate of interest is small or non-existent (as we shall argue that it is, on the basis of empirical evidence) this does not argue *in favour* of the efficacy of monetary controls (as the adherents of the quantity theory of money would have it) but on the contrary, of the impotence of the monetary authorities to vary the quantity of money otherwise than in response to variations in demand. On this view the close correlation between the quantity of money and the level of income is proof, not of the *importance* of monetary policy, but of precisely the opposite, the variation in the stock of money being no more than a reflection of the change in the volume of money transactions. The greater the response of the 'money supply' to changes in the volume of money transactions, the less is there a need to economize on money; and this is the explanation of the apparent paradox that the supply of money and the velocity of circulation are often found to move in the *same* direction, instead of in opposite directions.

---

of the public for liquidity which depends both on incomes and on the rate of interest, i.e. r determines the relevant point on the demand curve for money.

[48] The reason for this probably was that by the 'rate of interest' he invariably meant the *long-term* rate of interest (as measured by, say, the yeild of Consols) whilst the interest paid on time deposits, under the cheap money regime prevailing in the 1930s, was $1-1\frac{1}{2}$ per cent *below* the Bank Rate, and hence something quite negligible.

[49] See H. G. Johnson, 'Monetary Theory and Policy', *American Economic Review*, 1962, pp. 344–5.

C. *The interest elasticity of money*

73. Table III and Figure I show for the United Kingdom and the United States the change in the volume of demand deposits and interest-bearing time deposits for the years 1963-78, expressed as a percentage of GNP, and the prevailing short-term interest rates for those years. The definition of interest-bearing deposits in this table is broader than that included in the statistics of the United States for M2 or in that of the United Kingdom for M3, and includes savings deposits with non-bank deposit-taking institutions such as building societies. In both countries the trend of interest rates was upwards and they both show an inverse correlation between M1 (interest-free deposits) and the interest rate; the movements over time in both countries (and the magnitude of the ratios to the GNP in the two countries) are remarkably similar, thus confirming Keynes's hypothesis that the higher the sacrifice of interest the more people wish to economize on money balances. The interest-elasticity of these balances, however, is not very large; the demand for money as a proportion of income fell by about one-third in a period in which the short-term interest rate more than doubled (indicating an elasticity which is much less than unity).

74. With interest-bearing deposits, on the other hand, it was the other way round; with the rise of the interest rate, balances increased as a percentage of income, and this increase has more than offset, in both countries, the decline of non-interest-bearing balances. Hence the net effect of interest changes on a broad definition of the 'money stock' was perverse — a rise in interest rates appears to have led to the 'money stock' rising faster than money income, not lagging behind it. On the basis of the historical experience of these two countries, the Central Banks' habit of using interest rates as a regulator of the money supply[50] appears singularly inept — higher interest rates tend to *increase* the 'money supply' and not decrease it. Any positive effect of reducing growth of the money supply could only come about as a consequence of the decrease in total savings resulting from lower real incomes and employment; it is doubtful, however, whether taking interest rates alone (i.e. ignoring fiscal measures) the effects — within the range of variation that is considered feasible from the point of view of business solvency — would be powerful enough to lead to lower monetary growth. And if they did, this occurrence would not really signify

[50] See the Mais Lecture of the Governor of the Bank of England, published in *Bank of England Quarterly Bulletin*, March 1978.

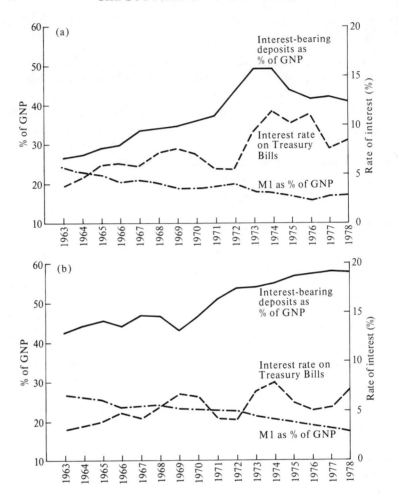

Fig. I. Variations of money and interest rates, 1963–78.
(a) United Kingdom table
(b) United States table

anything about the *modus operandi* of monetary controls. For it would not mean that any lessening of inflation occurred in *consequence of* lower monetary growth; on the contrary, any slow-down in the growth of the 'money stock' would be the consequence of a reduction in total incomes, and hence in the volume of savings, some part of which is lodged in bank deposits.

TABLE III

Interest rates and the demand for interest-free and interest-bearing deposits in the United Kingdom and United States

(per cent)

	1963	1964	1965	1966	1967	1968	1969	1970	1971	1972	1973	1974	1975	1976	1977	1978
United Kingdom																
Interest rate on Treasury bills (average for year)	3.7	4.6	5.9	6.1	5.8	7.1	7.6	7.0	5.6	5.5	9.3	11.4	10.2	11.1	7.7	8.5
Ratio of M1 (mainly interest-free) to GNP	24.2	23.0	22.3	20.5	21.0	20.1	18.8	18.7	19.2	19.9	18.0	17.6	16.8	15.7	16.7	17.1
Ratio of other bank deposits plus private savings deposits with non-bank deposit-taking institutions[1] to GNP	26.6	27.3	29.0	29.8	33.3	34.1	34.6	35.8	37.2	43.5	49.1	49.3	43.6	41.5	42.1	40.8
United States																
Interest rate on Treasury bills (average for year)	3.2	3.6	4.0	4.9	4.3	5.4	6.7	6.4	4.3	4.1	7.0	7.9	5.8	5.0	5.3	7.2
Ratio of M1 (mainly interest-free) to GNP	26.7	26.0	25.3	23.5	23.9	24.1	23.1	23.0	22.6	22.4	21.2	20.3	19.7	18.7	18.0	17.1
Ratio of other bank deposits plus private savings deposits with non-bank deposit-taking institutions[1] to GNP	42.4	44.2	45.5	44.0	46.9	46.6	43.0	46.7	50.9	53.6	53.9	54.9	56.6	57.3	57.8	57.6

[1] In the United Kingdom the non-bank deposit-taking institutions are Building Societies. In the United States, they are Savings Banks, Saving and Loan Associations, and Credit Unions. As these institutions hold bank deposits, there is a small element of double counting in these figures.

Sources: International Financial Statistics, various issues; Bank of England Statistical Abstracts Nos. 1, 2; Financial Statistics.

D. *The income elasticity of money*

75. Tables IV–VI show comparisons of the rise of the money stock in relation to GNP for ten industrial countries and their movement over time for three different definitions of the money supply: the narrow definition (M1) shown in Table IV, the usual broad definition (M3) which includes the interest-bearing deposits of clearing banks, shown in Table V, and finally, in Table VI, the 'broadest' definition, which comprises all deposits (including those with non-bank deposit-taking institutions) is so far as they are statistically available. (The figures for the United States and the United Kingdom in this table are the same as the sum of the two series shown in Table III.)

76. A study of these tables confirms the impression gained when I first studied the level and movement of the velocity of circulation (which is the reciprocal of the ratio of the money stock to the GNP) in preparing my evidence to the Radcliffe Committee in June 1958.[51] I then wrote that 'in some communities the velocity of circulation is low, in others it is high, in some it is rising and in others it is falling, without any systematic connection between such differences and movements and the degree of inflationary pressure, the rate of increase in monetary turnover, etc.'[52] The present tables, which relate to a subsequent period, bear out the same conclusions as the earlier study. Taking the 'narrow' definition of money, the figures show a falling trend in most countries, with the notable exception of Italy and Japan, where the period 1958–78 had shown a remarkable rise in the ratio (i.e. a *fall* in the velocity of circulation) despite the fact that these were two countries with the highest rates of increase in money GNP, and possibly of inflation, as well.[53] This is in contrast to the 'age old experience' that in a prolonged inflation the velocity of circulation *rises*, as people get accustomed to it and begin to anticipate it.[54] All other countries in Table IV (with the exception of Germany where the ratio remained remarkably stable) show a fall in the ratio (i.e. a rise in velocity) which

[51] See Committee on the Working of the Monetary System, *Principal Memoranda of Evidence*, Vol. 3 (HMSO, 1960) pp. 146 ff.

[52] Ibid., p. 146. In the attached footnote I gave the figures of the ratio of the money supply to the GNP and its movement over time for a number of (developed and developing) countries.

[53] The figures show for 1958–78 an annual rate of growth in income of 12 per cent for Italy, of which 7.4 per cent represented inflation, and 14 per cent for Japan, of which 5.2 per cent was due to price-inflation.

[54] See F. A. Hayek, letter to *The Times*, 31 May 1980.

TABLE IV

Ratio of narrow money supply (M1) to nominal GNP in ten industrial countries (in percentages)

Country	1958	1962	1966	1970	1974	1978	Change in ratio 1958–78 (per cent)	Increase in money supply 1958–78 (per cent)	Increase in GNP 1958–78 (per cent)
Belgium	40.2	39.3	37.2	29.3	26.1	25.9	–35.6	279.6	491.6
France	31.2	35.6	35.5	29.5	29.4	26.5	–15.1	648.0	780.5
Germany	17.1	16.4	15.1	15.1	15.1	17.6	2.9	470.0	454.0
Italy	30.0	38.3	41.0	53.0	58.3	55.6	85.3	2058.0	1065.8
Japan	22.6	27.0	31.8	29.1	33.3	33.4	47.8	2546.0	1690.5
Netherlands	28.2	27.0	24.4	22.5	20.6	21.2	–24.8	490.7	686.1
Sweden	12.8	13.7	12.8	10.4	11.6	10.7	–16.4	423.8	525.8
Switzerland	52.9	53.9	47.3	48.7	38.2	48.2	–8.9	354.0	398.1
United Kingdom	n/a	n/a	20.5	18.7	17.6	17.1	–16.6[1]	251.0[1]	320.8[1]
United States	31.6	27.1	23.5	23.0	20.3	17.1	–45.9	153.4	367.6

[1] Changes are for 1966–78

Sources: International Financial Statistics, various issues; Bank of England Statistical Abstract No. 2.

TABLE V

Ratio of broad money supply (M3) to nominal GNP in ten industrial countries (in percentages)

Country	1958	1962	1966	1970	1974	1978	Change in ratio 1958–78 (per cent)	Increase in broad money supply 1958–78 (per cent)	Increase in GNP 1958–78 (per cent)
Belgium	46.1	47.9	47.6	45.1	45.0	47.1	2.2	503.6	491.6
France	33.4	40.4	42.5	43.7	50.9	51.2	53.3	1247.4	780.5
Germany	36.0	38.0	43.5	52.0	58.0	67.0	86.1	930.8	454.0
Italy	51.9	67.2	73.0	82.3	92.6	96.5	85.9	2068.3	1065.8
Japan	49.6	69.3	80.2	73.8	81.1	86.6	74.6	3029.9	1690.5
Netherlands	44.7	48.5	46.7	49.3	52.1	58.8	31.5	933.9	686.1
Sweden	35.7	35.4	32.7	32.2	41.3	38.2	7.0	570.4	525.8
Switzerland	98.5	106.3	103.4	118.6	99.8	125.9	27.8	536.6	398.1
United Kingdom	40.6	37.5	35.0	34.8	44.8	34.9	−14.0	499.7	596.8
United States	45.5	43.9	43.6	45.9	49.1	45.3	−0.4	365.0	367.6

Sources: International Financial Statistics, various issues; Bank of England Statistical Abstracts, Nos. 1 and 2.

TABLE VI

Ratio of broadest money supply[a] to nominal GNP in eight industrial countries (in percentages)

Country	1958	1962	1966	1970	1974	1978	Change in ratio 1958–78 (per cent)	Increase in broadest money supply 1958–78 (per cent)	Increase in GNP 1958–78 (per cent)
Belgium	58.9	62.2	60.8	57.4	56.7	59.5	1.0	496.3	491.6
France	44.0	53.0	58.1	61.8	71.3	74.3	68.9	1386.0	780.5
Italy	60.8	77.2	83.1	91.2	102.2	100.0[b]	64.5[b]	1546.8[b]	901.7[b]
Japan	n/a	n/a	n/a	93.1	105.6	116.1[b]	9.9[bc]	216.3[bc]	153.5[bc]
Netherlands	57.1	62.9	60.6	62.1	63.4	71.1	24.5	879.2	686.1
Sweden	67.2	68.0	64.3	63.1	n/a	n/a	−6.1[d]	157.1	173.6
United Kingdom	51.3	49.8	50.3	54.5	66.9	57.9	12.9	687.0	596.8
United States	64.4	66.7	67.5	69.7	75.2	74.7	16.0	442.5	367.6

n/a not available.
[a] Money plus quasi-money plus savings deposits with other deposit-taking institutions. Since the latter hold deposits with commercial banks there is some element of double-counting in these figures. No figures for other deposit-taking institutions are provided in *International Financial Statistics* for Germany and Switzerland, which are therefore excluded from the table.
[b] 1977 figures are used rather than 1978 figures.
[c] Change for period beginning 1970.
[d] Change for period ending 1970.
Sources: International Financial Statistics; Bank of England Statistical Abstracts Nos. 1, 2; Financial Statistics.

was largest in the case of the United States, Belgium, and the Netherlands, and significant in Sweden and the United Kingdom. There are remarkable differences *between* countries in the ratios themselves (varying between 85.6 per cent for Italy to 10.7 per cent for Sweden) which are difficult to explain since these figures refer to cash in hand plus current accounts, the demand for which depends on the factors determining 'transaction velocity' – which in turn supposedly reflects the frequency of income payments and of regular out-payments (for rent, gas, electricity, etc.) – factors in which the habits of different countries cannot be so different from each other. The figures for 1978 show in fact remarkable similarities for three countries (i.e. United States, United Kingdom, and Germany), but why should the income-velocity of circulation be five times as high in Sweden as it appears to be in Italy or in Switzerland?

77. The figures for M3 show a similar range of variations *between* countries, but the general trend is upwards, not downwards (only the United Kingdom shows a significant decrease in the ratio over the last twenty years), and the highest increases shown are for Germany (whose rate of inflation was one of the lowest) as well as for Italy and Japan (whose inflation was among the highest). The explanation probably is that interest-bearing bank deposits are a popular form of saving in some countries, so that the increase in deposits in relation to income shows the effect of the accumulation of personal savings, some proportion of which are held in this form. Some support for this hypothesis is shown by comparison with Table VI which shows that in the case of Italy money on the 'broadest' definition (which includes in addition deposits with savings banks, building societies, etc.) was very little larger, as a proportion of income, than the 'broad' definition which includes only bank deposits; while in the case of Japan the proportional difference due to the addition of such deposits was less than in the case of the United States and the United Kingdom, which latter show a trend increase in the 'broadest' definition, but not in the 'broad' definition. On the other hand there are countries which show a strongly rising trend on both definitions (France and the Netherlands) and those who do not show such a trend on either definition (Belgium and Sweden).

78. I cannot pretend to explain these wide-ranging differences in both the level and the time-trend of the ratio of money to income, whatever definition is chosen. The fact that differences appear substantial on the 'broadest' definition as well as on the 'narrower' definition suggest to me that they cannot be explained simply in terms of

differences of classification, or even differences in saving habits or in the velocity of circulation due to differences in the frequency of income payments or in the settlement of debts. They rather suggest that money, contrary to the fashionable view, is an 'unimportant' quantity — if the Swedes are content with so much *less* money than the Swiss, for example, this may be due to nothing more important than historical accident which made the public of one country become used to having so much larger cash balances than that of another. It certainly does not suggest that the plenitude of money of the Swiss makes them *more* inflation-prone than the 'sparseness' of money which characterizes the Swedes or the British (of all people!).

E. *The myth of the time-lag*

79. The common article of faith of all monetarists is that changes in the money supply affect inflation with a time-lag, which is normally taken to be two years. Thus the Minister of State in the Treasury (Lord Cockfield) assured the House of Lords on numerous occasions that: 'there can be no doubt, based on both theory and practical experience that a growth in the money supply is followed after a period of time by a rise in the rate of inflation, and equally, and more hopefully, that a fall in the rate of growth of money supply is also followed in due time by a fall in the rate of inflation.'[55]

80. Almost identical statements were made by the Chancellor and Treasury Ministers on numerous previous occasions. Prior to the formation of the present Government, the same assertion was made by various economists and writers, among them Mr W. Rees Mogg in *The Times* of 16 July 1976. The basis of this assertion was that the inflation of the years 1974-5 was correctly 'predicted' by the increase in the money supply which occurred two years earlier, in 1972-3.

81. As Table VII shows, the average annual percentage increase in £M3 in the five years 1971-6 in the United Kingdom 'predicted' the average annual increase in the money value of the GNP between 1973-8 (that is to say, two years later) with quite remarkable precision: the average percentage difference between the two series was only 0.23 per cent. But Table VII also shows that this was a unique occurrence; it was not true of the United Kingdom either for the preceding period 1963-8, or for the succeeding period 1975-8, for both of which the closest fit is shown when *no* time-lag is assumed. The same is true for the average of the nine other countries in the table which show that, in

[55] House of Lords, *Official Report*, 11 June 1980, col. 517.

the large majority of cases, the best fit is obtained when no time-lag is assumed, for all three periods shown. There are a few isolated cases in which the postulate of a two year lag shows a smaller discrepancy — such as Germany in 1963–8, but here the discrepancy between the money series and the GNP figures is so large in relation to the total (4.5–5.25 per cent according to the time lag assumed, with a GNP rise of only 7.25 per cent) that it is difficult to attach any significance to the fact that one lag gives somewhat better results than another. The same is true of Switzerland, in the case of which the gaps are insignificant for all three money-series for the period 1963–8, but are enormous for all three series in both the 1973–8 and 1975–8 periods — the percentage growth of the money supply being over twice as large as the percentage growth of the money GNP in all three cases.

82. Clearly the United Kingdom figures for the middle period, 1973–8 — a discrepancy of only 0.23 per cent with a two-year lag, but 3.29 per cent with a one-year lag and 5.71 per cent with no lag — are a pure fluke. They are the accidental result of the dominating influence of two events which were themselves wholly unrelated to each other; the adoption of the system called 'Competition and Credit Control' by the Bank of England in 1971 and the Arab–Israeli War (the so-called Yom-Kippur War) of October 1973 which resulted first in an oil embargo on certain countries and then in a fourfold rise in the world oil price, which in turn induced the world-wide inflation of the years 1974–5.

83. We shall discuss the consequences of the change in banking rules below. Here we merely wish to note that the large increase in the money supply (£M3) by 58 per cent was mainly due to the increase in interest-bearing time deposits (which increased by 117 per cent in two years whilst sight-deposits, M1, increased only by 19.5 per cent). This terrific 'bulge' in interest-bearing deposits was largely the consequence of banking policy changes — the clearing banks, freed from control, successfully diverted funds from normal channels and indulged in, or tolerated, a great deal of financial manipulation (e.g. the so-called 'round-tripping' by which money borrowed from one bank is re-deposited in another). There was no conceivable connection between these events and the large world-wide inflationary wave induced by the 'oil shock' of 1973, which had particularly grave consequences on the severity of inflation in the United Kingdom in 1974, on account of the 'threshold' arrangements (these were part of Phase 3 of the Heath Government's income policy but fixed before the big oil price rise) which, by the end

TABLE VII
Average annual growth rates of the money supply (M3) and GNP

Country	M3			GNP	M3			GNP	M3			GNP
	1961-6	1962-7	1963-8	1963-8	1971-6	1972-7	1973-8	1973-8	1973-6	1974-7	1975-8	1975-8
Belgium	8.49	8.50	8.34	8.43	13.33	11.86	10.60	11.32	12.12	12.23	9.73	9.60
France	12.57	11.49	10.99	8.87	15.84	14.93	14.52	13.75	15.27	14.07	13.03	13.63
Germany	11.92	12.55	13.54	7.23	11.71	10.66	10.46	6.87	10.61	10.80	9.76	7.45
Italy	14.17	13.39	13.08	9.33	20.47	21.33	21.25	21.68	20.35	22.55	22.08	20.90
Japan	19.19	18.34	15.97	16.54	16.11	13.46	12.73	12.78	13.15	13.01	12.56	11.51
Netherlands	10.13	10.74	11.32	11.33	15.38	14.99	14.05	10.76	15.44	14.27	13.77	10.50
Sweden	8.16	8.44	9.30	8.95	14.07	13.09	13.56	12.25	14.15	7.31	9.27	10.82
Switzerland	8.87	8.19	8.68	8.90	6.70	6.30	7.30	3.14	6.71	6.93	7.72	2.78
United Kingdom	5.17	6.77	6.92	7.61	17.10	13.58	11.16	16.87	10.52	9.48	11.94	15.74
United States	7.51	8.11	8.90	8.02	9.44	8.90	8.76	10.24	7.93	7.95	9.29	11.65

Average percentage differences (without regard to sign) between changes in M3 and GNP	1963-8 Period			1973-8 Period			1975-8 Period		
	Two-year time-lag	One-year time-lag	No time-lag	Two-year time-lag	One-year time-lag	No time-lag	Two-year time-lag	One-year time-lag	No time-lag
United Kingdom	2.44	0.84	0.69	0.23	3.29	5.71	5.22	6.26	3.80
All countries, excl. UK	2.05	1.75	1.59	2.70	1.79	1.76	2.83	2.74	1.93
All countries, incl. UK	2.09	1.66	1.50	2.45	1.94	2.15	3.07	3.10	2.12

Sources: IMF International Financial Statistics; Bank of England Statistical Abstracts.

of 1974, nearly doubled the inflation rate as compared with what would have happened otherwise.[56] Thus the remarkably rapid rise of the money supply in 1972-3 and the rapid inflation two years later were a pure coincidence which had no parallel in any earlier or later period. Of the thirty observations recorded in Table VII (i.e. for each of ten countries for three different periods), in nineteen cases the closest 'fit' was obtained when *no* time-lag was assumed (i.e. when both the money series and income series related to the *same* period) a one-year lag gave the 'best fit' in four cases and a two-year lag in seven cases; but with the sole exception of the United Kingdom for 1973-8, none of these 'exceptions' appears significant; either the difference in the closeness of fit is too small (as for example for Switzerland in 1963-8), or else the fit is so poor in all three cases (e.g. for Switzerland in 1973-8 or Germany in 1963-9) as to make any conclusion drawn from them highly suspect. There is certainly nothing in these figures that would justify the far-reaching and confident assertions of Treasury Ministers about the existence of a significant time-lag, which, as was repeatedly asserted, is based on 'empirical evidence' or 'practical experience'.

F. *Present UK monetary policy*

84. The core of the economic philosophy of the present Treasury Ministers is that 'public expenditure is at the heart of Britain's economic difficulties.'[57] because it is the cause both of excessive taxation and of the large borrowing requirement, which in turn is the real cause of inflation because it is responsible for an increase in the money supply which is the immanent cause of the rise in prices.

85. All this is best summarized by the statement made in January 1980 by the Financial Secretary of the Treasury (Mr Lawson):

Let me start with two simple facts. The first is a statistic. The PSBR is at present about $4\frac{1}{2}\%$ of total gross domestic product (GDP) — compared with an average of only $2\frac{1}{2}\%$ in the 1960's. The second is an economic relationship. That is, the PSBR and the growth of the money supply and interest rates are very closely related. Too high a PSBR requires either that the Government borrow heavily from the banks — which adds directly to the money supply; or, failing this, that

---

[56] As a result of the rapid rise in prices in the first four months, shots of the 'trigger' started in April rather than in September–October (as originally expected).

[57] Cmnd. 7746, 1979, para. 1.

it borrows from individuals and institutions, but at ever-increasing rates of interest, which place an unacceptable squeeze on the private sector.

86. There are two assertions here: one, that the PSBR and the growth of the money supply are closely related; and two, that to avoid too fast an increase in the money supply requires borrowing from individuals and institutions (as distinct from banks) which in turn can only be accomplished at 'ever increasing rates of interest'.[58] It is best to deal with these two contentions separately.

(a) *The PSBR and the growth of the money stock* 87. The assertion which forms the central thesis of the Government's economic philosophy that public sector borrowing is 'the major cause of the growth of the money supply' is without any empirical foundation whatsoever and could only be made by someone in total ignorance of the facts, as set out in official statistics by the Treasury and the Bank of England.

88. The relevant figures and relationships show, in my view quite conclusively, that Mr Lawson's assertions concerning 'simple facts' are not facts at all but fairy-tales effectively contradicted by the statistics shown in Table VIII.[59]

89. On Mr Lawson's hypothesis the PSBR causes a corresponding increase in the money supply unless it is 'funded' — i.e. unless the money is borrowed from individuals and institutions through the net sale of securities to the public. In the latter case the budget deficit is financed by 'genuine savings', and therefore it is non-inflationary; but it creates an 'unacceptable squeeze on the private sector' by 'crowding out' productive investment.[60] The part of the PSBR which 'adds directly to the money supply' is therefore the part which is *not* funded in this way and this is shown in column (3) of the table. This shows that for the last three financial years such 'unfunded borrowing' was virtually zero — it amounted to £390 millions for the three years taken together which is the equivalent of *less than* 0.1 per cent of the GDP for that

[58] There is, of course, an implied third assumption, that an excessive growth in the money supply is the direct cause of inflation, but this has already been dealt with in previous sections.

[59] 1973 and earlier years are given on a calendar basis owing to difficulties in obtaining comparable figures for the money supply on a quarterly basis. However from 1974/5 onwards the figures are shown in terms of financial years which give a more reliable indication of the change in the PSBR from one financial year to the next and its relation to the national income as measured by GDP at factor cost.

[60] On this question of 'crowding out' see paras. 105–26.

TABLE VIII

The PSBR, funded and unfunded, and changes in the money stock

	(1) PSBR	(2) Net acquisition of public sector debt by UK non-bank private sector (funded PSBR)	(3) (1)–(2) Unfunded PSBR	(4) Changes in sterling money stock M3	(5) PSBR as % of GDP	(6) Unfunded PSBR as % of GDP	(7) Unfunded PSBR as % of changes in money stock	(8) Annual growth in £M3
	£m.	£m.	£m.	£m.				%
Financial years								
1979/80	9789	9085	704	6449	5.9 est.	0.4 est.	10.9	12.4
1978/79	9282	8537	745	5285	6.4	0.5	14.1	11.4
1977/78	5597	6656	−1059	6233	4.3	−0.8	−17.0	15.5
1976/77	8523	7190	1333	2829	7.5	1.2	47.1	7.5
1975/76	10585	5230	5265	2453	10.8	5.4	214.6	7.0
1974/75	7993	4220	3773	2738	10.1	4.8	137.8	8.5
Calendar years								
1973	4182	2094	2088	6702	6.5	3.3	31.2	26.3
1972	2040	1007	1033	4927	3.7	1.9	21.0	24.5
1971	1373	2104	−731	2455	2.8	−1.5	−29.8	13.4
1970	−17	102	−119	1541	0.0	−0.3	−7.7	9.7
1969	−466	359	−825	374	−1.2	−2.1	−220.6	3.0
1968	1279	−13	1292	1072	3.4	3.4	120.5	7.2
1967	1863	665	1198	1252	5.3	3.4	95.7	10.6
1966	961	262	699	446	2.9	2.1	156.7	4.1
1965	1205	486	719	915[1]	3.9	2.3	78.6[1]	7.6
1964	989	504	485	597	3.4	1.7	81.2	5.2
1963	842	594	248	697	3.1	0.9	35.6	6.5

[1] 1965 and before, M3 statistics on different basis.

Source: *Financial Statistics.*

period. Over the same period the increase in the money supply (£M3) was £18.0 billions or forty-six times as large. In other words the unfunded PSBR, assuming that all of it was financed by bank credit (some of it may have been financed by net overseas purchases) could only have contributed 2.1 per cent to the increase in the money supply. Its influence, therefore, since April 1977, was completely negligible.

90. On the other hand if one takes the preceding three years, when the PSBR, as a percentage of the GDP, was nearly twice as large (it averaged 9.5 per cent of GDP as against 5.5 per cent in the last three financial years) the 'unfunded' borrowing requirement was £10.4 billions, or twenty-six times as large as in the subsequent three years and was indeed 29.6 per cent greater than the *total* increase in the money supply in that period.

91. Yet the increase in the money supply over the three years 1974/5-1976/7 was only £8.1 billions, or less than one-half as large as in the three years 1977/8-1979/80 when there was practically *no* public sector borrowing from the banking system.

92. Indeed a brief glance at columns (7) and (8) of Table VIII is in itself a complete disproof of the theory underlying the Government's medium-term strategy as expounded in Part II of the *Financial Statement and Budget Report 1980-81*, according to which 'there is no doubt that public sector borrowing has made a major contribution to the excessive growth of the money supply in recent years'. Taking the last six years as an indication of 'recent years', the size of public sector borrowing which was not 'funded' by the net sale of securities to the UK private non-banking sector fluctuated from 214.6 per cent of the growth of the money supply (in the financial year 1975/6) to −17.0 per cent (in 1977/8). Yet the growth of the money supply was lowest − at 7.0 per cent − in the financial year 1975/6 when unfunded PSBR was at its highest, and it was highest − at 15.5 per cent − in the year 1977/8 when the 'unfunded' PSBR was actually negative. Moreover the extreme variation in 'unfunded' borrowing − from +214 per cent to −17 per cent − is in such complete contrast to the narrow range of variations in the year-to-year growth of the money stock (from 7.0 per cent to 15.5 per cent, averaging 10.4 per cent for the six years) as to rule out the possibility of the one series exerting an influence on the other. If the Government's factual assertions were correct, and public sector borrowing was a 'major cause' of the growth of the money supply, column (8) would have varied year by year, in sympathy with column (7). There is no evidence of that whatsoever; if anything there

was a perverse relation between the two in which the highest 'unfunded' PSBR was associated with the lowest growth in the money stock, and vice versa. The 'Barber years' seem to show a somewhat different picture, but the explanation of that does not lie in the size of uncovered public sector deficit but in the uncontrolled growth of bank lending to the private sector of those years, which occurred for reasons explained below. This makes complete nonsense of the assertions made in this year's *Financial Statement* according to which the planned reduction in the growth of the money supply will depend on the 'path for the PSBR'.[61] If past experience is any guide — and what else is there to go on? — it will have nothing whatever to do with that factor.

93. A comparison of the *whole* of the PSBR (both funded and unfunded) ought to be better related to the change in the money stock, since the latter should be in some relation to the growth of the money national income, and the PSBR is one of three major components determining the growth of demand (the others are the net loan expenditures of the private sector and the balance of payments on current account). The figures in Table VIII however, do not support that view either. The years in which the PSBR, as a proportion of GDP, was very large — such as the two years 1974/5, 1975/6 and also 1976/7 — the growth of the £M3 as a percentage of the total money stock was particularly low as compared with both earlier or later years, while in the years when PSBR was relatively low (such as 1977/8, 1972, and 1971) the percentage growth in £M3 was relatively high.[62]

---

[61] Para. 14.

[62] I myself believed at one time (see my paper on 'The New Monetarism', *Lloyd's Bank Review*, July 1970, p. 16) 'that the basic relationship between money and income (i.e., that the change in the "money supply" is a reflection of the change in money incomes) is modified in the short period by the behaviour of the income–expenditure relation (or, as I would prefer to call it, the receipt–outlay relation) of those particular sectors whose receipt–outlay relation is particularly unstable — in other words, whose dependence on "outside finance" is both large and liable to large variations — for reasons *which are endogeneous, not exogeneous to the sector* [italics in the original] . . . [this] is true of the public sector whose "net borrowing requirement" has been subject to very large fluctuations year by year' (as a consequence of Keynesian economic management which varied the receipt–outlay relation of the public sector deliberately so as to stabilize the growth of effective demand). The idea was eagerly seized on by Milton Friedman and other economists who said from then on that Governments are the chief culprits in inflation because, wishing to avoid unpopularity, they spend too much and tax too little. Subsequent history has shown, however, that I was wrong (and so, of course, was Friedman) — while there was a correlation between the PSBR and the growth of M3 for the period 1954–68, it disappeared *completely* afterwards, as the regression equations in Table X show.

TABLE IX

The 'sources' of growth of the money stock

	(1)	+	(2)	+	(3)	equals	(4)
	PSBR unfunded		Bank lending in sterling to UK private sector		Net overseas finance to UK, expressed in sterling		Change in money stock £M3
Actual change, in £m.							
1979	1798		8556		-3771		6583
1978	2324		4698		-250		6772
1977	-2462		3188		3404		4130
1976	3364		3464		-3263		3565
1975	4935		-371		-2233		2331
1974	3210		3435		-3390		3255
1973	1903		5972		-1173		6702
1972	1041		5510		-1624		4927
1971	-731		1576		1610		2455
1970	-119		1135		525		1541
1969	-820		525		669		374
1968	1292		570		-790		1072
1967	1198		577		-523		1252
1966	699		53		-306		446
Change, expressed as % of change in money stock							
1979	27		130		-57		100
1978	24		69		-4		100
1977	-60		77		82		100
1976	94		97		-92		100
1975	212		-16		-96		100
1974	99		106		-104		100
1973	28		89		-18		100
1972	21		112		-33		100
1971	-30		64		66		100
1970	-8		74		34		100
1969	-219		140		179		100
1968	121		53		-74		100
1967	96		46		-42		100
1966	157		12		-69		100

Source: Financial Statistics, CSO, May 1980 (and earlier).

94. If the PSBR, whether funded or unfunded, thus cannot account for the changes in the money stock, how are the latter to be explained? Table IX accounts for the annual growth in the money stock for the years 1966-79 in terms of three 'sources': (1) the unfunded part of the PSBR; (2) bank lending to the United Kingdom private sector; (3) net overseas finance to the UK. These three elements together are so defined as to be equal to the annual change of £M3 (the first two elements have in recent years come to be called 'domestic credit expansion'). It should be emphasized that as the table represents an identity it can say nothing about causality. It is equally consistent with the monetarist view according to which an increase in the money stock is fully 'explained' by public or private sector borrowing *plus* net overseas finance (which provides a source of finance for borrowing only when the balance of payments on current account is unfavourable). But it is also consistent with a non-monetarist view according to which the change in the money stock and the size of bank lending may both be determined by other factors — such as the increase in total expenditures which in turn are to be explained by autonomous changes in private investment, by the rise in money wages, the propensity to consume, etc. But on the monetary view the three sources can be taken as 'explaining' the change in the money stock which in turn is taken as 'explaining' whether inflation takes place and, if so, by how much.

95. It will be evident from a glance at the table that the unfunded part of the PSBR (which in turn is equal to the public sector's borrowing from the banking system *plus* the net issue of notes and coins) can have played only a minor role in the change in the money stock, whereas bank lending to the UK private sector played the major role. This is formally proved in the regression equations in Table X which show the contribution of each of the three factors separately, as well as the sensitiveness of bank advances to the private sector of bank lending to the public sector (i.e. the banking system's absorption of public sector debt). These regression equations show conclusively that the role of the unfunded PSBR was quite insignificant; it explains only 5 per cent of the change in £M3 in the last fourteen years. As against that, bank lending in sterling to the UK private sector is the factor that was overwhelmingly responsible for the change in the money stock, as it explains 83 per cent of the change. Finally, the last regression equation shows that bank finance to the private sector has not been influenced by the banks' absorption of public sector debt.

Table X. *Contributions to the growth of £M3 1966-79*

$$\Delta M3 = 2903.0 + 0.27\ (PSBR\text{--}F)$$
$$(751.6)\ \ (0.34)$$
$$R^2 = 0.05$$
$$\Delta M3 = 1065.6 + 0.78\ BA$$
$$(390.5)\ \ (0.10)$$
$$R^2 = 0.83$$
$$\Delta M3 = 2989.5 - 0.32\ NOF$$
$$(662.0)\ \ (0.32)$$
$$R^2 = 0.08$$
$$BA\ \ = 2589.5 + 0.15\ (PSBR\text{--}F)$$
$$(890.2)\ \ (0.40)$$
$$R^2 = 0.01$$

Definitions:
$\Delta M3$ = change in £M3
(PSBF--F) = the unfunded element of the public sector borrowing requirement
BA = bank lending in sterling to UK private sector
NOF = net overseas finance to the UK
Notes: Figures in parentheses are standard errors. Equations are estimated by ordinary least squares.

96. These regression equations offer a complete disproof, within their own realm of discourse, of the main contentions on which the present Government's economic strategy is based, as explained in numerous speeches of Ministers and in Part II of the *Financial Statement and Budget Report, 1980-81.*

(b) *The PSBR and interest rates*   97. So much for Mr Lawson's first contention. His second contention stands up no better than the first. This asserts that to avoid the inflationary consequences of the PSBR, the Government must borrow 'from individuals and institutions, but at *ever-increasing rates of interest*, which place an unacceptable squeeze on the private sector'.

98. First of all, which rate of interest had he in mind? There is the short-term rate of interest, now called MLR, which governs the rate on Treasury Bills, and the rates obtainable on interest-bearing deposits repayable at short notice with banks or other deposit-bearing institutions. And there is a whole spectrum of long or medium term interest rates, measured by the redemption yield of gilts of varying maturity, or by the flat yield of perpetual bonds (like $2\frac{1}{2}$ per cent Consols). In

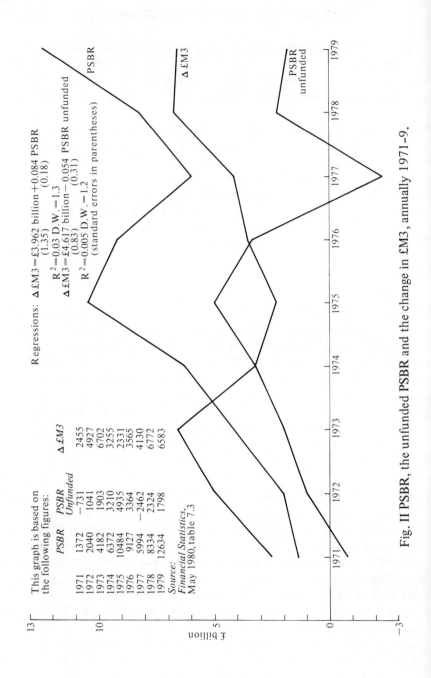

This graph is based on the following figures:

	PSBR	PSBR Unfunded	Δ£M3
1971	1372	−731	2455
1972	2040	1041	4927
1973	4182	1903	6702
1974	6372	3210	3255
1975	10484	4935	2331
1976	9127	3364	3565
1977	5994	−2462	4130
1978	8334	2324	6772
1979	12634	1798	6583

Source:
Financial Statistics,
May 1980, table 7.3

Regressions: Δ£M3 = £3.962 billion + 0.084 PSBR
                                   (1.35)   (0.18)
$R^2 = 0.03$ D.W. = 1.3
Δ£M3 = £4.617 billion − 0.054 PSBR unfunded
                    (0.83)   (0.31)
$R^2 = 0.005$ D.W. = 1.2
(standard errors in parentheses)

PSBR

Δ£M3

PSBR
unfunded

£ billion

Fig. II PSBR, the unfunded PSBR and the change in £M3, annually 1971–9.

'borrowing from individuals and institutions' by means of the sale of Government securities what matters is the *additional yield* which has to be offered on such securities as compared with the current rate of interest on bank deposits (or Treasury Bills) and the expected future short rates of interest during the lifetime of the security issued. For the cost to the buyer of purchasing long- or medium-term securities is the sacrifice of *foregone liquidity* (and not the sacrifice of *foregone consumption*). Savings out of personal income are largely contractual in character: it is for this reason that such a large part of personal savings is channelled through institutions like insurance companies and pension funds as well as deposited in savings banks and building societies. It is not a question therefore of *inducing* individuals to save (in the sense of inducing them to refrain from current consumption), but only of inducing them to commit themselves to a purchase of a long-term security which is subject to the risk of a capital loss (as well as to the chance of a capital gain) on account of future changes in the rates of interest. It has been calculated that the additional yield of long-term Government securities over the seven-year moving average of short-term rates (which was used as a proxy for *expected* short-term rates) was 1 per cent prior to 1913 and around 2 per cent in the period between the two wars.[63] At present (in May 1980) there is a large and widespread *negative* yield gap (i.e. one extending to short and medium dated stock, as well as the pure long-term rate) between gilts and the Minimum Lending Rate, which must be an indication of the public expecting both short- and long-term interest rates to *fall*. In fact despite the present Government's unexpected increase in the MLR to 14 per cent in June and then to 17 per cent in November, the yield of long-dated gilts is well *below* their yield in 1974–5, when the interest rates were barely above 12 per cent. Gilt-edged yields are the same as in the third quarter of 1978 and are only a little higher (by about $1\frac{1}{2}$ per cent) than in the summer of 1979, when they were exceptionally low in the expectation of a reduction of MLR. And indeed they have not risen much in consequence of the wholly unexpected rise of the MLR to 17 per cent. During all that time there was a flood of new issues which offset over 90 per cent of the PSBR; in the last financial year the flood became a veritable torrent, with net new issues for cash yielding £11.5 billions, or twice the amount in the previous financial year.

[63] See J. R. Hicks, 'Mr Hawtrey on the Bank Rate and the Long-Term Rate of Interest', *Manchester School*, Vol. X (1939), p. 31.

99. Since April 1975, when the yield of $2\frac{1}{2}$ per cent Consols was over 15 per cent, the Government borrowed (net) from individuals or institutions – i.e. the non-bank UK private sector – the modest sum of £36,788 millions, or 84 per cent of the cumulative PSBR of £43,776 millions of the last five financial years. The current yield of Consols is just under 12 per cent or 3 per cent lower. In relation to the MLR, which was $9\frac{3}{4}$ per cent in April 1975, and is now 17 per cent, the *fall* in the yield of Consols was 7 per cent. So much for the contention that the PSBR can only be funded 'at ever increasing rates of interest'.

100. To be accurate, Mr Lawson should have said that the Government has been able to borrow from individuals and institutions in almost unlimited amounts at redemption yields which are on a downward trend and are much lower now than those offered in earlier years (with the exception of a six-month period in 1977–8 and another such period in 1979–80) and at an *ever-increasing negative yield gap* between those yields and interest on Treasury Bills, which the Government keeps deliberately high for the express purpose of 'squeezing' the private sector.

101. For it is the Government-imposed MLR, and *not* the gilt-edged yields determined by future interest expectations, which are solely responsible for the 'squeeze' on company finance. If heavy borrowing from individuals and institutions required 'ever increasing interest rates' we would have had a situation in which the upward-pull of long-term rates dragged the short-rate up behind it; instead of which the wholly policy-imposed level of the MLR, even though it has been kept up for nearly a year, failed to shake the public's expectations that future interest rates will be much lower than now, and that they are *bound to fall heavily soon* – otherwise there could not exist a large negative yield gap even as between short-dated securities repayable within a few years.[64] ‡

102. How is this to be squared with the importance attached by all monetarists to 'inflationary expectations'? On the monetarist view the current rates of interest (on loans of any particular duration) should correspond to Fisher's 'real' rate of interest *ex ante*, i.e. it should make an allowance for the expected rise in prices during the currency of the loan. Since the current rate of inflation is 20 per cent, the yield of $11\frac{1}{2}$ per cent on short-dated gilts must therefore imply, on the theory of

[64] [For subsequent developments see p. 112.]

monetarists, the prevalence of 'deflationary' expectations which alone explain why such yields should be so much less than the rate of increase in prices.

103. However, there is a fallacy here which is no less damaging to clear thinking for being widely believed, even among economists who do not subscribe to the monetarist creed. This consists of the proposition that the *expected* rise in prices enters into the supply-price of loans — i.e. that people are not willing to part with 'liquidity' except at a price (in terms of redemption yields) which makes allowance for the expected rise in prices until the redemption date, in addition to the 'normal' return on that particular type of loan. This view is false for the simple reason that the holding of liquid financial assets (which is the alternative to holding bonds) is exposed to exactly the same risk of erosion in real value through inflation as gilts are. Inflationary price expectations therefore do *not* enter into the determination of interest rates for loans of differing duration: these are solely determined by expected *interest rates*, both long and short (which must be consistent with one another). The expectation of a rise in prices, as Keynes maintained, will raise the 'marginal efficiency of capital' but it will not affect the current yield of bonds, except in so far as it also carries with it the expectation of higher short-rates of interest in the future. A negatively-sloped yield curve in the London market necessarily implies that people expect that *both* short and long rates will fall; but this does not imply (or not necessarily) that they also expect prices to fall, or even that they expect the rate of increase in prices to diminish. The two are not necessarily linked to one another, except on the supposition that people expect the Government to go on raising the MLR in the vain hope that this in itself will bring inflation to an end, sooner or later; in that case, however, they ought to expect *rising* interest rates in the future, the expectation of which would imply a large positive yield gap, and not a negative one.

104. The rate of interest (MLR) is the one instrument which is entirely under the control of the Government.§ It is the declared policy of the Bank of England to use it as the prime regulator of the money supply; for that purpose, however, it is a particularly inept instrument, since, as we have seen, the direct effect of a rise in MLR is to increase the growth of the money stock and not to decrease it (as it makes interest-bearing deposits *relatively* more attractive). For regulating the 'money supply' the Government is mainly dependent on 'funding' which in turn is very much a matter of creating — and maintaining —

the expectation of *falling* interest rates. Keeping MLR at very high rates (such as 17 per cent) is good for the money supply mainly because people cannot believe that it can last, and the longer it lasts the less they appear to believe (rationally or irrationally) that it can continue at that level. This alone explains why investors appear to be increasingly bullish on gilts, even though the yield on long-term issues already discounts a reduction in MLR that is of a far greater magnitude than is likely to happen in the foreseeable future, for reasons explained below.

G. *Crowding out*

105. One frequent contention of the monetarist school — though it figures less prominently in recent official pronouncements — is that public sector borrowing, if funded, 'crowds out' private sector borrowing. This view, to my mind, ignores:

(*a*) the role of the PSBR as a regulator of the level of economic activity — whether as a 'built-in stabilizer' which changes automatically in inverse relation to cyclical changes in activity, or as an actively used instrument of demand management (as was the case up to 1973);

(*b*) the reason why the PSBR is capable of fulfilling this role, which lies in the dependence of the *volume* of savings on the level of income, which is the fundamental axiom of Keynesian economics. As activity increases (with higher employment and a higher utilization of capacity), savings increase more than in proportion to the increase in income, owing to the close connection between savings and profits. At low levels of capacity utilization the *share* of profits is very low, mainly on account of high overheads per unit of output (whether of labour costs, rents, etc., or interest payments) and the cash flow may be insufficient to provide for increased working capital requirements on account of higher wages and higher fuel and material prices. This necessitates additional borrowing for the replacement of stocks, the interest burden of which may reduce net profits even further. But if economic expansion was renewed unit costs would fall with the expansion of activity, and a disproportionate share of the improvement in incomes would go into profits and therefore savings.

106. For the same reason a reduction of the PSBR attained through expenditure cuts of higher taxes, or both, will reduce activity further and this will be attended by a disproportionate reduction in savings.

Hence the savings which are theoretically 'freed' by the reduction in public borrowing will not be there when the borrowing is cut – on the contrary, as savings will fall more than in proportion to the fall in incomes there will be less savings than before available to the economy.

107. So instead of 'crowding out', there is, on the supposition that the level of activity varies with effective demand, a 'crowding in' effect – the savings available for private investment will vary in direct relation with the PSBR and not in an inverse relation.

108. This conclusion may be modified if the balance of payments effects of changes in the PSBR are taken into account. To the extent that the expansion of demand resulting from large Government expenditure or lower taxes goes on imports, the additional incomes, and hence the additional savings, will accrue to foreigners. (This, I presume, is what the Chancellor had in mind by saying that the British economy is hemmed in by 'supply difficulties'.) In such circumstances a reduction in the PSBR may cause a reduction in imports rather than in home output; but on that assumption it is not an efficacious method for reducing the rate of inflation, which requires a reduction in home output and employment. The assumptions under which public borrowing 'crowds out' private borrowing are the same as those under which home output cannot be either stimulated or depressed by fiscal or monetary measures. *21/329*

109. There is finally the question of the role of Government borrowing in inflation (discussed in the paper by C. T. Taylor and A. R. Threadgold).[65] Since inflation necessarily redistributes wealth from creditors to debtors, and since the public sector is a net debtor and the private sector a net creditor in terms of financial assets, the erosion of private wealth resulting from inflation can only be prevented by maintaining the 'gearing' of publicly owned assets – i.e. by the Government maintaining current borrowing at the level required to keep the aggregate value of the National Debt as a proportion of the total national wealth unchanged. This argues in favour of *lower* taxes and *more* borrowing in times of inflation – which is the very opposite of the usual prescription based on the view that inflation is caused by too much borrowing and too little taxation. The answer turns, like everything else in the monetarist–anit-monetarist controversy, on whether the inflationary process is viewed as one of excess demand or whether it is viewed as a political process – a tug-of-war between different factions and opposing interest for larger slices of the national cake –

[65] Bank of England Discussion Paper No. 6.

a war that is likely to become more acute the smaller the cake is, and the less it grows (or the more it shrinks).

110. An inflation of prices resulting from excess demand brings its own cure – since the resulting rise in prices will proceed to the point at which real disposable incomes are reduced to a level at which the available supplies are no longer insufficient to satisfy demand. For inflation to continue as a *process* in time it is necessary therefore that money incomes should be continually replenished, more or less in line with the rise in prices; in which case, however, we are faced with a cost-induced inflation that can proceed irrespective of whether the underlying *real* situation is one of excess supply or excess demand. In a sense all inflationary processes that proceed in time, that is to say which do not peter out of their own accord, are cost-induced inflations: they reflect the failure of society to distribute its real income in a manner that is acceptable to the great majority of its inhabitants.

111. Continued inflation causes an erosion of the wealth of the *rentier* class which directly or indirectly owns the National Debt, in favour of the State – which means the community as a whole. Whether this process is regarded as good or bad is a prima facie political question which does not admit a single 'right' answer. But whatever views one takes on the merits of the question, it should be pointed out that the interests of the *rentier* class are not necessarily served best by choosing the most orthodox financial policies. If the inflationary process is not a consequence of excessive Government borrowing, but proceeds more or less independently of the size of the PSBR, the best policy, from the point of view of the property-owning classes, is one which keeps taxes low enough in relation to expenditure to offset the erosion in the real value of the National Debt by current additions to the Debt.

112. This of course should not be regarded as the sole or even the most important consideration in determining 'the desirable trend path' of the PSBR. The latter raises all the considerations involved in securing an optimal utilization of resources, and the best long-term strategy in terms of economic growth, the balance of payments, etc.

H. *Inflation and the personal savings ratio*

113. Several economists of the monetarist' school (among them Messrs Ball and Burns of the London Business School and Professor Patrick Minford of Liverpool) put forward the theory that inflation, and particularly inflationary expectations, are responsible for the spectacular rise in the personal savings ratio from the customary 8-9 per cent (up

to 1972-3) to 14-15 per cent from 1974 onwards — or in terms of *net* financial savings (net of investment by persons and un-incorporated businesses) from 4-5 per cent to 9-10 per cent. This reasoning is that people wish to maintain intact the real value of their accumulated savings; as they are eroded through inflation, they increase the proportion of savings out of current income on order to offset this.[66] It followed from this view that if inflationary expectations were broken by the Government's publishing a medium-term target for the rate of monetary growth, this would serve to balance the reduction in the net demand effect resulting from a lower PSBR with the expansionary effect of a lower personal savings ratio — so that, by getting rid of the public sector deficit, inflation could be stopped without any increase in unemployment (which would otherwise have resulted from the reduction in the public sector's net demand for goods and services).[67]

114. Unfortunately, none of these authors appear to have taken the trouble to investigate the causes of the change in the savings ratio by looking at the various components which make up the net financial savings of the personal sector. If they had done so, they might have taken a different view on the causes of the change in personal savings.

115. The analysis of the change of savings ratio by the movement of various components over time is shown in Table XI which gives figures for all years from 1959 to 1978. It is seen that there was an abrupt rise in the personal savings ratio from 1974 on. Total financial savings as a percentage of personal disposable income hovered around 3-4 per cent in the years 1963-73. But in 1974 they rose to 8.4 per cent and have since remained at that level and even rose slightly further to 9.7 per cent in 1978. Since double-digit inflation became chronic around 1972-3, the hypothesis that savings jumped when people became accustomed to the continuance of inflation at this rate appears a priori plausible.

116. However, it finds little support when one examines the component series of personal savings. There are items like life assurance and superannuation funds which show a fairly steady upward trend throughout the period irrespective of inflation. There are others such as notes and coins and bank deposits and Government debt, which show annual fluctuations but *no* trend. The series which appears to have been responsible for the sudden break in the figures is the residual item

[66] If this theory were correct, it would of course greatly strengthen the case for maintaining an inflation-adjusted PSBR so as to avoid the deflationary effects of a higher savings ratio.

[67] See e.g. P. Minford's article in *The Times*, 4 February 1980.

'other' which is consistently negative, but which during the three Barber years 1971-3 was (numerically) twice as large as either before or since — averaging +15 per cent in 1971-3 against +7 per cent both before and after that period. As the table shows, the greater part of increase in the identified items (which account for around four-fifths of the total residual) is accounted for by the rise in consumers' credit and in loans for house purchases, and the rest by the higher net sale of company and overseas securities of the personal sector. All three of these items were unusually large (numerically) during the three 'Barber years' — twice as large as in the preceding or in the succeeding years. The large rise in consumer credit and loans from house purchases reflects the credit explosion following 'Competition and Credit Control' which came to a sudden halt with the imposition of the 'corset' late in 1973. But the increase in the personal sector's net sale of company and overseas securities in those years is presumably offset — to an unknown extent — by the increase in bank deposits (which are also unusually large for those years) in which case it indicates a shift in the distribution of portfolios of individual shareholders (which is presumably offset by opposite change in the portfolio holdings of institutions).

117. The rise in net personal financial savings by 3.4 percentage points between 1973 and 1974 can be more than fully accounted for by the 5.6 percentage points reduction in 'dis-savings' in the form of new consumer credit and mortgages. This clearly had nothing to do with inflation or the anticipation of inflation, for that should have caused people to *increase* their borrowing for such purposes, and not to reduce them. And looking at all the other components in the table there is nothing in any of the series which would provide the slightest support for the theories advanced by the London Business School or Professor Minford — indeed I am sure they would never have advanced these views if they had taken the trouble to look at the dis-aggregated figures readily available in the National Income Blue Book.

J. *Alternative methods of controlling the money supply*

118. Under the pre-World War I gold standard, control over the money supply was relatively easy, since even small changes in relative interest rates between financial centres (such as London and New York) brought about large changes in the liquidity of the banking system, on account of the flow of funds induced by interest rate changes. After World War I, this system never worked in the same way — presumably because the risks of exchange rate variations (or of devaluation through

TABLE XI

Personal Sector Transactions in Financial Assets,[1] as a percentage of Personal Disposable Income

	1959	1960	1961	1962	1963	1964	1965	1966	1967	1968	1969	1970	1971	1972	1973	1974	1975	1976	1977	1978
Net Acquisition of Financial Assets	0.1	1.9	3.4	2.8	2.7	3.2	3.8	4.0	3.3	1.8	2.3	3.8	1.2	2.4	4.5	8.4	9.4	9.2	8.4	9.7
of which																				
Notes and Coins and Deposits with Banks	2.7	1.4	1.2	1.5	1.8	2.3	2.4	1.1	2.9	2.0	1.2	2.7	2.8	4.5	7.1	5.5	1.9	1.9	1.1	3.4
Other Deposits[2]	1.6	1.2	1.1	1.9	2.3	2.2	2.7	2.8	3.9	3.1	3.2	4.8	5.7	5.6	4.6	3.4	5.9	4.1	6.7	4.8
Funds with Life Assurance Companies and Superannuation Schemes	4.2	4.5	4.4	4.6	4.9	4.9	4.7	4.7	5.0	5.1	4.7	4.9	5.5	6.7	6.7	6.1	6.1	6.6	6.5	6.8
Government debt	2.8	4.4	2.1	2.4	1.3	1.7	1.1	0.8	0.1	-0.5	0.3	-1.0	1.5	0.8	2.1	2.0	1.6	3.0	2.3	1.5
Other	-11.2	-9.6	-5.4	-7.6	-7.6	-7.9	-7.1	-5.4	-8.6	-7.9	-7.1	-7.6	-14.3	-15.2	-16.0	-8.6	-6.1	-6.4	-8.2	-6.8
of which																				
Bank Advances and Credit from Retailers	-3.2	-1.5	-0.1	-0.8	-0.7	-1.2	—	0.7	-0.6	-0.1	0.4	-0.3	-1.4	-4.7	-2.1	-0.1	0.5	-0.9	-1.2	-1.7
Loans for House Purchase	-2.1	-2.1	-1.9	-2.0	-2.6	-3.2	-2.8	-2.9	-3.6	-3.3	-2.7	-3.6	-4.7	-6.3	-5.5	-3.9	-4.9	-4.5	-4.4	-4.7
Company and Overseas Securities	-2.2	-2.1	-1.6	-1.9	-2.6	-2.8	-3.1	-2.2	-2.5	-2.4	-1.6	-2.4	-3.5	-3.4	-4.4	-1.9	-1.3	-1.8	-1.8	-1.4

[1] Acquisition of assets or reduction of liabilities is shown positive; sale of assets or increases in liabilities negative.
[2] Deposits with savings banks, building societies, and other societies, and other financial institutions.
Source: National Income and Expenditure, 1979, 1970.

changes in the gold parity) were never ruled out altogether; and after 1931, the management of the 'money supply' required different policies and different instruments for each country. However no serious problems arose until the late 1930s, since the cheap money policy of the main financial centres was not sufficient to lead to a full reactivation of resources, and almost until the outbreak of World War II, the risk of inflation was not taken seriously in Britain.

119. During the war, apart from extensive rationing and price controls of consumer goods, there was also rigid credit control imposed on the banks who were obliged to redeposit all surplus funds with the Treasury (the so-called Treasury Deposit Receipts). The main control instrument was the regulation of the amount of credit that banks were permitted to extend to the private sector, and priorities were laid down in the allocation of bank lending.

120. With periodic tightening and relaxation, such quantitative controls over bank advances were retained even after 1951 when an active interest rate policy was reintroduced as an instrument of regulating credit. The Radcliffe Committee concluded that credit control through interest rates was almost wholly ineffective beyond causing a 'diffused difficulty of borrowing'. They therefore approved the use of quantitative ceilings on bank advances and hire purchase controls as an effective remedial measure in 'emergencies'. With the return of the Labour Government in 1964 quantitative control of bank advances became the dominant form of credit control. However there was increasing criticism of these methods on the ground that they diverted business to smaller banks and to overseas banks which were not subject to control; and also that the controls limited the growth of each bank not just absolutely but in relation to each other and thereby limited 'competition' between the clearing banks. Various schemes were considered to permit freer competition between banks.[68]

121. However, the scheme actually adopted by the Conservative Government in 1971, 'Competition and Credit Control' was based on the idea that by creating an inter-bank wholesale market for loans,

[68] The Labour Government of 1964–70 considered a scheme of introducing a 'public sector lending ratio' (of 50 per cent or some other percentage) which would have had the effect that each particular bank could only extend credit to the private sector in proportion to growth of its holding of public sector debt, and since the Government could control how much public sector debt is made available to the banking sector as a whole, this would have enabled the Government to exercise a global control on loans to the private sector without limiting any individual bank's freedom to increase its market share.

with individual banks freely bidding for funds both as borrowers and lenders, the best results will be obtained at a rate of interest (established by the market) which equates the demand and supply for loanable funds. The authors of this plan failed to take into account that the 'loan market' is different from other markets in that the banks, in their anxiety to expand their business, went in search of borrowers and thus used the facilities of the newly established wholesale 'deposit market' to balance their creation of bank assets (i.e. those resulting from additional lending) with an artificial increase in their liabilities, by actively bidding for wholesale deposits – leading to phenomena such as that known as 'round tripping' whereby a company or a financial institution could obtain a loan from Bank A (anxious to extend its lending business) on terms that made it profitable to on-lend to Bank B who was anxious to acquire additional liabilities to match the expansion of its assets. So far from the system leading to a new equilibrium between the demand and supply for loanable funds, it led to a scramble between banks to expand their operations on *both* the asset and liability side as fast as possible. The resulting inflation of bank credit – which I believe I am right in thinking was quite unexpected both by the Bank and the Treasury – led to a rapid expansion of interest-bearing liabilities of the banks, and of credit extended to customers for speculative purposes, which created a rapid and unhealthy boom in the property market.[69] Mortgages became very easy to get, with the result that house prices nearly doubled in a period of a few months, and there was wild speculation in property companies as well as an unhealthy growth of 'secondary banking' which the new system was originally intended to discourage. The rise in house prices was rapidly passed backwards into increased land values – which had a perverse effect on building activity, since it caused landowners to hold on to potential development land, thereby increasing the shortage of development land still further.

122. At the end of 1973, the Government found it necessary to put a brake on this feverish process of speculation and credit expansion[70]

[69] As already mentioned above, the introduction of the new system led to a rise of interest-bearing deposits of 112.5 per cent between the end of 1971 and 1973, whereas previously the annual increase was of the order of 5–10 per cent a year.

[70] This was done partly by the development land tax which imposed a charge on the increase in the value of development land which could, in certain circumstances be levied even when the land was not actually sold; and by introducing a new system of penalties (which became popularly known as 'the corset') on banks which increased their interest-bearing eligible liabilities in excess of the permitted rate.

which in turn led to a spectacular collapse of 'secondary banking', and made it necessary for the Bank of England to organize a scheme in co-operation with the main clearing banks (called the 'lifeboat') which at the cost of many hundreds of millions of pounds succeeded in averting the occurrence of bank failures which could have rapidly swollen into a financial panic of nineteenth-century style. After that the 'corset' was employed, on and off, in order to limit the rate of expansion of bank credit, but since this system was increasingly evaded by transferring 'liability management' to subsidiaries — and also by the banks' willingness to remain in the penalty areas and pay for it, which they could easily afford to do, given the abnormal size of bank profits resulting from high interest rates — the Bank abolished the corset altogether on 19 June 1980, and at the time of writing is back in the situation in which it found itself at the end of 1971.[71]

123. However, the experience of using interest rates as the central instrument for the control of monetary aggregates has not been a happy one. In those sectors of the economy where prices are cost-determined — as in manufacturing industry — the interest cost of working capital is part of prime costs, and is therefore passed on in prices in much the same way as a rise in labour cost. However, unlike a rise in wages, the rise in interest rates has no counterpart in increased spending; it thus acts in the same way as an increase in taxation which serves to reduce the fiscal deficit. And where circumstances are such that the rise in interest charges cannot be passed on (for reasons discussed in paras. 39 and 57 above) it eats into profits; with continually rising rates, this is bound to lead to a situation where firms become insolvent for lack of cash to pay interest on their loans, or where they have to borrow in order to pay interest on previous borrowing, a process that is sure to lead to bankruptcy.

124. In my view the change of policy which meant using the MLR and money market rates primarily for regulating the monetary aggregates has been a foolish and unimaginative innovation which is bound to be abandoned sooner or later for reasons discussed in the next section. Of course control is necessary to prevent an undue explanation of credit to the private sector, particularly for speculative purposes

[71] The so-called Reserve Asset Ratio (which became meaningless since the banks, with the aid of the discount market, could manufacture reserve assets) was abolished at the same time, so that there is no limit on credit expansion at present other than a 'prudential' cash ratio of some 2 per cent which however can also be replenished if necessary through the discount market by re-discounting eligible securities with the Bank of England.

or for consumer credit. But for this purpose it is best to go back to some improved and more comprehensive version of the lending controls abandoned in 1971.[72] The argument about 'lack of competition' between the clearing banks or between the clearing banks and other banks, does not seem to carry much weight; there are only four large banks left, so the situation is one of 'oligopoly' in any case; and large and persistent borrowers could maintain accounts and secure over-draft facilities with several banks simultaneously.

125. Failing this there are two other measures that might be considered for adoption. The first is putting a ceiling on interest rates which banks can pay on time deposits – a British version of 'Regulation Q'. The disadvantage of this is that it could lead to increased 'disintermediation' – the technical term for arranging finance outside the banking system, mainly through trade credit.

126. The other is to introduce a variable public sector lending ratio, such as was considered in the 1960s. Assuming that the authorities can control the amount of public sector debt made available to the banking sector (this may require confining 'eligible debt' to bills or short-term bonds which are not normally held in large amounts by the non-banking public) this might provide an effective instrument for controlling bank lending to the private sector as a whole, without limiting the rate of expansion of any single bank, taken individually.

3. THE PROBLEM OF EXCHANGE RATE POLICY

127. Throughout the 1960s there was a fairly general consensus among economists that the exchange rate of the £, at the parity of $2.80 fixed after the devaluation of 1949, became too high in the changed circumstances of the late 1950s and the 1960s; that it was as a result of this that our export performance (as shown by the rapid fall in our share of world trade in manufactures) was unsatisfactory; and that this in turn was a severe handicap on our economic progress as compared with countries such as Germany, Italy, or Sweden, whose economic growth was 'export-led'.[73]

[72] Most European countries employ controls on bank lending to regulate the money supply.

[73] Export-led growth was superior to 'consumption-led' growth (achieved as a result of Keynesian policies of economic management) partly because the latter engendered a weak balance of payments position, with the growth of imports always tending to outrun the growth of exports, necessitating 'stop-go' policies to protect the balance of payments; but mainly because it meant that the scope

128. Guided by these considerations I became a strong advocate (in the 1960s) not just of devaluation, but of the adoption of a 'managed' exchange rate (such as Keynes advocated in 1924) – in other words, a formally floating exchange rate, but where the rate was managed by market intervention so as to maintain an adequate stimulus to our manufacturers to secure a certain target rate of growth of exports. As is well known, there were strong political objections to devaluation of any kind, as a result of which this move was delayed well beyond the time when it might have arrested an irretrievable loss in our long-established position in numerous foreign markets; and when this move was finally forced on the Government in 1967, it occurred too late to bring about a lasting improvement in our international competitive situation. Though the Government, under the Chancellorship of Mr Jenkins, introduced unprecedented increases in taxation to secure the necessary resources for a rapid expansion of exports, the stimulus petered out after some years, and under the succeeding Conservative Government the priorities were again reversed in favour of a fiscally engineered boom based on rising domestic consumption demand.

129. So when a Labour Government returned in 1974, it was faced both with an inflationary wave in world prices unleashed by the oil price explosion of December 1973, and by a built-in acceleration of wage-inflation due to the operation of the 'threshold' arrangements under the final phase of the previous Administration's statutory incomes policy, which provided that all wages and salary payments were automatically adjusted each month once the retail price index exceeded by more than 7 per cent its October 1973 level. On account of the unexpectedly large rise in world prices this critical phase was reached in April (whereas, as originally envisaged, this would not have occurred much before September) and from then on both wages and prices were 'hiked' each month by at least 1 per cent and sometimes by 2 per cent. As a result of this, whereas at the beginning of the year the rate of inflation in Britain was not greatly out of line with those of her competitors, by November 1974 (when the 'threshold' arrangements came to an end) the rate of inflation in Britain of both wages and prices was almost twice that of her competitors. The maintenance of inter-

for the expansion of manufacturing industry was so much less than with countries enjoying export-led growth, and it was the growth of manufacturing industry which held the promise of improvements of productivity due to the introduction of new techniques, new industries, and the exploitation of economies of scale.

national competitiveness required that the exchange rate of the £ should be adjusted downwards — which was a difficult thing to do since any engineered reduction in the exchange rate could unleash widespread speculation against the £ which would be difficult to contain with the resources available. Hence the Treasury and the Bank followed a cautious policy which consisted of 'creaming-off' the day-to-day fluctuations in the market — by selling sterling against foreign currencies in moderate amounts whenever the demand exceeded the supply, thereby moderating the rise in market value, while not resisting a fall in the exchange rate by sales of foreign currency during periods when supply exceeded the demand. This policy was pursued fairly successfully in the course of 1975 and early 1976, though our competitiveness did not wholly regain its 1974 level until after March 1976 when the £ became subject to international bear-speculation and fell further and faster than was desired by the authorities — indeed at times it looked as if its excessive fall would generate strong inflationary forces. It was only after successful negotiations with the IMF over the activation of higher credit *tranches* that there was a sudden change in 'confidence' and the authorities were again in control of the situation. In the course of 1977 the operation of the Government's incomes policy — which brought down the annual increase in earnings in manufacturing industry from 31.8 per cent in the first quarter of 1975 to 8.7 per cent in the third quarter of 1977 — meant that the world-wide bear-speculation of 1976 turned into a world-wide bull-speculation in 1977 (aided also by rapidly improving North Sea oil prospects) which the Government resisted by not permitting the dollar exchange to rise above the rate that was considered appropriate from the point of view of our competitiveness — a rate of depreciation of 61.8 per cent of the Smithsonian average (or roughly $1.71 to the £) which was maintained unchanged for the first three quarters of the year,¶ despite a net inflow of foreign currency which averaged, in the first half of 1977, £750 millions a month. This flow grew to the dimensions of a flood in September and October of that year when dealings became so hectic that on some days several hundred millions worth of foreign currency was bought by the authorities in a matter of hours.

130. The Government responded to this persistent inflow in the traditional manner by lowering MLR, which had stood at $14\frac{1}{2}$ per cent in early January 1977, in successive steps reaching 8 per cent in July, 7 per cent in August, 6 per cent in September and 5 per cent at the end of October. Still the money continued to flow in, and the

Government were faced with the choice of either lowering the rate still further — there was still a long way to go before the traditional minimum of 2 per cent — or giving way to speculators and letting the rate float upwards.

131. In the light of the general 'monetarist' atmosphere — which regarded an inflow of foreign money as dangerously inflationary, not to speak of the 'unsoundness' of 'absurdly' low money market rates — the Chancellor was evidently persuaded that this situation could not be allowed to continue.[74] So the decision was taken to 'de-cap' the pound (as the move was then called) and allow it to float freely upwards; with some slight ups and downs and minor interruptions this has gone on ever since. But it entailed that as the pound became increasingly overvalued, the current balance of payments went into the red again despite increasing recession and despite the steady improvement in oil account. It entailed moreover that the exchange rate and the interest rate moved in tandem, so to speak, to make our economic prospects increasingly bleak. Every rise in the MLR served to make the exchange rate higher than it would have been otherwise, every rise in the exchange rate required higher interest rates, lest a change in sentiment brought about a dreaded exchange crisis.[75]

132. A high and rising exchange rate is recommended by monetarists as the principal method by which high interest rates and/or restraint in the growth of the money supply exert a 'downward pressure' on prices. From October 1977 on until May 1979, sterling's effective change rose by 7.8 per cent; since the new Government came into office it rose by a further 9 per cent, but this did not prevent a further increase in the rate of increase in wages and prices which is now [in June 1980] almost twice as high as in the average of other industrial countries. So at the moment, the pound is grossly overvalued in terms of competitiveness.

133. But however overvalued the pound is, it is always dangerous

---

[74] With 1·4 million unemployed and the balance on payments of current account only just coming out of the red (it was —£425 million a quarter in the first two quarters and +£500 million a quarter in the last two quarters) the danger of the economy being 'poisoned' by an excessive increase in currency reserves was remote in the extreme. The important factor was that after many unsuccessful years the £ was at last stabilized at a level which, with the continuance of a successful incomes policy, would have made it possible to initiate a period of soundly-based export-led growth.

[75] A good example of this was the sudden drop of the exchange rate by 5 cents when some remarks of the Prime Minister were interpreted by the market as presaging a reduction in the MLR. It was soon followed by a flood of official denials which quickly restored the situation.

to let it go down; indeed, in a sense it is more dangerous, because speculative expectations become more entrenched the worse is our balance of payments performance. Given the fact that out sight liabilities to foreigners are still greatly in excess of our reserves, we are in a weak position to resist a strong speculative attack — in a weaker position than when it last occurred in 1976, on account of the fact that in the mean time exchange controls on UK residents have also been swept away, which makes the scope of bear-speculation considerably greater. If, on the other hand, we allowed the exchange rate to drop by more than a moderate amount, it would add a further twist to internal inflation which would replace the present wage/price spiral with a wage/price/exchange-rate spiral, which on past experience of other countries, contains far more powerful self-accelerating forces.

134. For this reason I would be chary of recommending any active policy concerning the exchange rate for the present, such as making it an 'alternative target to the money supply' (whatever that may be taken to mean). As a result of short-sighted and mistaken policies, we allowed the exchange rate to drift from a position of potential strength to one of great potential weakness — despite our prospect of higher oil revenues. But these mistakes cannot easily be undone by reactivating the policies of a gradual downward 'float' so as to regain and maintain the rate at a competitive level. The problem of competitiveness — vital to our manufacturing industry — could best be dealt with by having a separate exchange rate applicable to a specified and identifiable class of transactions only. But with the vast amount of liquid funds now floating around the world the possibilities of de-stabilizing capital flows are so large as to make it too risky to pursue a policy of manipulating the exchange rate itself with a view to restoring and maintaining competitiveness on trading account.‖

135. If we introduce a policy of a general freeze on prices and wages along the lines recommended in para. 43, and were also able to carry it successfully into effect and maintain it, the present effective exchange rate (in terms of the Smithsonian) is bound to become a 'competitive rate' sooner or later since it is not likely that other countries will be able to eliminate inflation by adopting the same kind of policies. Beyond that — assuming that we succeeded with the aid of an industrial strategy to regain our lost technological lead in a number of key industries and became leading exporters again — it might be to our advantage to allow sterling to appreciate so as to insulate the economy as far as possible from the inflationary trends in the world's economy.

136. All this of course is speculation about possibilities in the distant future. Its implication for the present is only that it is best to avoid any hasty commitment for maintaining a fixed parity with other countries, as would be involved in joining the EMS, for example.

NOTES ON SUBSEQUENT DEVELOPMENTS
Added in February 1982

* (p. 58) Since the above was written, in June 1980, wage settlements in the manufacturing sector have come down substantially (from around 20 to 12 per cent p.a.) and the effective exchange rate of the pound has also fallen to a significant extent.

† (p. 59) It is only in these cases (i.e. where whole factories have closed down) that the rise in unemployment is likely to be accompanied by a rise in productivity, since the closures tend to be concentrated among enterprises of low productivity. This factor explains, I think, why the productivity record in the current recession was more favourable than could have been expected from the experience of earlier recessions.

‡ (p. 96) Since then, with the reduction to 12 per cent in March 1981, the negative yield gap has largely disappeared (except for very long-term issues), but has not yet been replaced by the 'normal' positive yield curve.

§ (p. 97) Since this was written MLR was officially abolished, in August 1981. I am assured, however, that *de facto* the Bank of England exercises the same control over money market rates as before.

¶ (p. 109) To be accurate, the Government's market intervention was aimed at stabilizing the dollar exchange up to June 1977, and at linking to the Smithsonian average after that.

‖ (p. 111) This was true at the time of writing. Since then, the deep recession of the economy has depressed imports, while oil revenue has become larger, so that the balance of payments on current account is now estimated to be in surplus by something of the order of £5–£6 billions a year. This of course makes the risk of a speculative attack on sterling very much smaller and the attraction of using the exchange rate weapon for improving competitiveness much greater.

INDEX

DATE DU